Abdulmanap Nurmagomedov

Abdulmanap Nurmagomedov

Cornerstone of Legacy

Alina Hazel

Mohammed Altaf Hussain

CONTENTS

Table of Content

Introduction: Beginnings of a Vision

1. Introduction to Abdulmanap Nurmagomedov's early life and upbringing.
2. Exploration of his passion for martial arts and the roots of his coaching philosophy.
3. Initial experiences in training and shaping aspiring fighters.

Chapter 1: The Nurmagomedov Dynasty

1.1 Overview of the Nurmagomedov family's rich martial arts history.

1.2 Abdulmanap's role in preserving and advancing the family legacy.

1.3 Anecdotes and stories showcasing the familial bonds and dedication to martial arts.

Chapter 2: Crafting Champions

2.1 In-depth examination of Abdulmanap's coaching techniques and training methods.

2.2 Highlighting the development of Khabib and other notable fighters under his guidance.

2.3 Interviews and insights from fighters who trained with Abdulmanap.

Chapter 3: Beyond the Octagon

3.1 Abdulmanap's contributions to martial arts beyond the world of MMA.

3.2 His involvement in community development and promotion of healthy lifestyles.

3.3 Exploration of his impact on the broader sports community.

Chapter 4: Triumphs and Challenges

4.1 Analysis of key moments in Abdulmanap's coaching career, including victories and setbacks.

4.2 Personal struggles and how he navigated challenges in the pursuit of excellence.

4.3 Examination of his resilience and determination.

Chapter 5: Legacy Beyond the Gym

5.1 Abdulmanap's influence on the cultural and social landscape of Dagestan and beyond.

5.2 Recognition of his efforts in promoting discipline, respect, and unity.

5.3 Testimonials from community members and leaders on his positive impact.

Chapter 6: Abdulmanap's Philosophies

6.1 Exploration of Abdulmanap's philosophical approach to martial arts and life.

6.2 Examination of key principles and values that shaped his coaching style.

6.3 Reflections on how these philosophies continue to resonate with fighters and fans.

Chapter 7: Remembering Abdulmanap

7.1 A tribute to Abdulmanap Nurmagomedov's enduring legacy.

7.2 Reflections from family, friends, and the MMA community on his lasting impact.

7.3 Examining how his teachings continue to inspire future generations of fighters.

Introduction

Beginnings of a Vision

Abdulmanap Nurmagomedov, a name inseparable from combative techniques greatness and a urgent figure in the realm of blended hand to hand fighting (MMA), set out on an excursion that would make a permanent imprint on the game. Naturally introduced to an unobtrusive family in the Republic of Dagestan, Russia, Abdulmanap's initial life was formed by the rough scenes and the champion ethos of his predecessors. It was in the midst of this setting that his vision for a day to day existence devoted to combative techniques started to flourish.

Since early on, Abdulmanap showed a characteristic liking for actual work and a strong fascination with the discipline of battle sports. Experiencing childhood in a locale with a rich history of wrestling and hand to hand fighting, he wound up attracted to the thorough preparation and the praiseworthy feeling implanted in these practices. As he improved his abilities, Abdulmanap's obligation to the quest for greatness became clear, establishing the groundwork for what might later turn into a celebrated profession in training.

The Nurmagomedov family, with its profound roots in hand to hand fighting, assumed an essential part in molding Abdulmanap's initial encounters. Encircled by a tradition of warriors and a culture that esteemed strength, discipline, and flexibility, he ingested the lessons of his progenitors. This familial impact turned into the foundation of Abdulmanap's way to deal with both life and combative techniques, imparting in him a significant feeling of obligation to convey forward the family's heritage.

As Abdulmanap's energy for hand to hand fighting increased, he dove into the complexities of different disciplines, from wrestling to judo and then some. His process was about self-awareness as well as about sustaining the capability of others. The seeds of his training reasoning were planted during these early stages, as he perceived the extraordinary force of mentorship and direction in the realm of battle sports.

The Nurmagomedov tradition, described by a heredity of heroes, turned into a point of convergence in Abdulmanap's life. It was an inheritance that he acquired as well as one that he tried to improve and give to people in the future. The family's obligation to combative techniques stretched out past the Octagon, making an embroidery woven with devotion, penance, and a common love for the quest for significance.

Abdulmanap's training process took off as he began forming the fates of hopeful contenders in Dagestan. The rec center turned into a pot for producing champions, and Abdulmanap's training ability started to draw consideration. Among his numerous protégés, one name would come to characterize his inheritance — Khabib Nurmagomedov. The connection among father and child rose above the run of the mill mentor competitor relationship, developing into an organization based on common regard, trust, and a common vision for significance.

Making champions was not just a quest for triumph in the enclosure for Abdulmanap; it was a comprehensive methodology that enveloped physical, mental, and otherworldly turn of events. His preparation techniques were thorough, stressing discipline, difficult work, and a profound comprehension of the essential subtleties of MMA. Contenders under his tutelage turned out to be genuinely considerable as well as embraced a set of rules that reflected Abdulmanap's own qualities.

Past the limits of the exercise center, Abdulmanap's impact reached out into the local area. He grasped the groundbreaking force of combative techniques in molding competitors as well as balanced people. His obligation to local area improvement and the advancement of solid ways of life became clear as he worked indefatigably to ingrain a feeling of satisfaction and reason among the young people of Dagestan.

Wins and difficulties interspersed Abdulmanap's training vocation. Triumphs in the MMA field were praised as individual accomplishments as well as aggregate victories for the Nurmagomedov heritage. In any case, the way to progress was not without deterrents. Abdulmanap confronted individual and expert difficulties, each trial of character met with steady assurance.

His strength despite affliction reflected the emotionless ethos imbued in Dagestani culture. Whether exploring the intricacies of the battle game or conquering individual mishaps, Abdulmanap's unflinching obligation to his standards stayed unshaken. These snapshots of challenge became necessary parts in the account of his heritage, displaying the triumphs as well as the fortitude fashioned in the pot of misfortune.

Abdulmanap's effect rose above the domain of MMA. His commitments to the more extensive games local area, both in Dagestan and then some, gained him appreciation as a figure of power and shrewdness. His direction was looked for by contenders as well as by hopeful mentors and sports lovers, every anxious to gather bits of knowledge from the one who had turned into a foundation of combative techniques greatness.

As the Nurmagomedov name acquired unmistakable quality in the realm of MMA, Abdulmanap remained grounded in his methods of reasoning.

His training went past specialized mastery; it was a comprehensive methodology that integrated components of discipline, regard, and lowliness. The exercise center was not only a preparation ground for warriors; it was a dojo where life examples were bestowed, and character was shaped.

Abdulmanap's methods of reasoning were established in the conviction that combative techniques was a way to self-revelation and self-awareness. The standards he imparted in his contenders went past the bounds of rivalry, pervading their daily existences. Regard for adversaries, lowliness in triumph, and elegance in shame were trademarks as well as lived encounters woven into the texture of his training heritage.

The inheritance Abdulmanap assembled stretched out past the rec center walls. His impact ventured into the social and social woven artwork of Dagestan, making a permanent imprint on the local area he called home. The qualities he supported — discipline, difficult work, and the quest for greatness — became core values for the vast majority, rising above the limits old enough and foundation.

The effect of Abdulmanap's lessons was felt by proficient warriors as well as by the endless people who embraced combative techniques for of individual strengthening. His rec centers became safe-havens where people from varying backgrounds discovered a feeling of direction and kinship. The people group turned into a demonstration of the persevering through tradition of a devoted his man life to the help of others.

As the years unfurled, Abdulmanap's lessons kept on resounding with contenders and fans the same. His insight, frequently conveyed in compact yet significant maxims, turned into a wellspring of motivation for those exploring the difficulties of life and game. Indeed, even as he turned into a respected figure, Abdulmanap stayed receptive, encapsulating the lowliness that characterized his instructing reasoning.

In 2020, the world bid goodbye to Abdulmanap Nurmagomedov. His passing was grieved not just by his family and the MMA people group however by a worldwide crowd that perceived the departure of a genuine visionary. The inheritance he abandoned, notwithstanding, perseveres in the hearts and psyches of those contacted by his lessons.

Recalling Abdulmanap isn't just a reflection on the past; a festival of an inheritance keeps on molding what's in store. His effect on MMA,

Dagestan, and the more extensive universe of combative techniques fills in as a demonstration of the getting through force of a dream brought into the world in the rough scenes of a district that fashioned champions. As we convey forward the illustrations of Abdulmanap Nurmagomedov, we become torchbearers of a heritage that rises above ages — an inheritance that stands as a foundation of combative techniques greatness.

1. **Introduction to Abdulmanap Nurmagomedov's early life and upbringing.**

   Abdulmanap Nurmagomedov, a name carved into the records of blended combative techniques (MMA), was not only a mentor or coach; he was a visionary whose effect stretched out a long ways past the limits of the octagon. To comprehend the man and the inheritance he created, one should dive into the pot of his initial life and childhood in the rough scenes of Dagestan, Russia.

   Brought into the world in 1962, Abdulmanap experienced childhood in a locale that had for quite some time been saturated with a practice of combative techniques and wrestling. Dagestan, settled in the North Caucasus, was not only a geological area for him — it was a pot that produced his character and molded his fate. The rich embroidery of Dagestani culture, with its accentuation on honor, flexibility, and actual ability, gave the background against which Abdulmanap's story unfurled.

   Brought up in an unassuming family, Abdulmanap's initial years were set apart by the difficulties intrinsic in a district described by its rough landscape and a background marked by hero tribes. It was an existence of straightforwardness, where the upsides of difficult work, discipline, and regard for custom were imparted since early on. These fundamental standards, imbued in the texture of Dagestani society, would turn into the bedrock of Abdulmanap's way to deal with life and combative techniques.

Since the beginning, Abdulmanap displayed a characteristic fitness for proactive tasks. The appeal of battle sports, profoundly implanted in the social legacy of Dagestan, brought him into the universe of wrestling. Wrestling, with its foundations in old practices, turned into a point of convergence for youthful Abdulmanap as he improved his abilities on the mats, submerging himself in the discipline and meticulousness of the game.

As a youngster, Abdulmanap saw the accomplishments of incredible Dagestani grapplers and military specialists who had become nearby legends. These figures, venerated for their solidarity and bravery, filled in as reference points of motivation for a young man with fantasies about transforming the universe of hand to hand fighting. The reverberation of strides on the mats and the aroma of sweat in the exercise centers turned into the soundtrack of his early stages.

The Nurmagomedov family, with its profound roots in hand to hand fighting, assumed a crucial part in forming Abdulmanap's initial encounters. Naturally introduced to a tradition of champions and contenders, he acquired a family name as well as a legacy of strength and a pledge to the quest for greatness. The family's military heredity, going back ages, turned into a wellspring of pride and obligation regarding Abdulmanap.

In the Nurmagomedov family, combative techniques was not only an occupation; it was a lifestyle. Family social events frequently spun around conversations of preparing regimens, stories of wins on the wrestling mats, and the insight bestowed by older folks who had explored the difficult way of a military craftsman. It was inside this familial setting that Abdulmanap's vision for his own process started to come to fruition.

The social scene of Dagestan, set apart by an embroidery of dialects, customs, and identities, gave an extraordinary background to Abdulmanap's early stages. It was a locale where the reverberations of old fights blended with the ordinary rhythms of life.

In this milieu, Abdulmanap's way of life as a Dagestani, with its conversion of ethnic variety and shared social qualities, turned into a necessary piece of his story.

As he explored the difficulties of immaturity, Abdulmanap's obligation to hand to hand fighting developed. The exercise centers, where sweat-drenched instructional meetings unfurled, turned into his safe-havens. The kinship produced in the pot of preparing was not just about actual effort; it was a holding of spirits joined by a common enthusiasm for the craft of battle. These early encounters laid the foundation for Abdulmanap's future as a mentor and coach.

In the complicated embroidery of Dagestani culture, wrestling held an exceptional spot. It was not only a game but rather a custom that rose above ages, a social relic passed down from father to child. For Abdulmanap, wrestling turned into a method for self-disclosure — a discipline through which he could channel his energy, develop discipline, and explore the intricacies of youthfulness.

The Dagestani ethos, profoundly interweaved with the Islamic confidence, bestowed a feeling of direction to Abdulmanap's excursion. The upsides of lowliness, regard, and determination, inborn in the lessons of Islam, were woven into the texture of his personality. The mosque, with its minarets coming to towards the sky, turned into an otherworldly anchor in Abdulmanap's life, giving direction and comfort as he outlined a course through the wild waters of youth.

Abdulmanap's youth harmonized with a time of international disturbance. The disintegration of the Soviet Association in the mid 1990s introduced a period of progress and change. Dagestan, winding up at the junction of history, wrestled with the difficulties of country building and the intricacies of character. Against this background, Abdulmanap's process reflected the versatility of his country — an excursion set apart by flexibility, determination, and an enduring obligation to his calling.

The charm of hand to hand fighting, in any case, rose above the boundaries of Dagestan. Abdulmanap's journey for information and dominance drove him to investigate different disciplines past wrestling. Judo, with its accentuation on procedure and influence, turned into a reciprocal feature of his preparation routine. The union of these different impacts established the groundwork for a training reasoning that would later shape the vocations of various contenders.

As Abdulmanap changed from the job of a hopeful competitor to that of a mentor, he conveyed with him the examples learned on the mats and in the recreation centers of Dagestan. His training reasoning, established in the standards of difficult work, discipline, and a profound regard for the customs of hand to hand fighting, started to come to fruition. The rec center became a preparation ground as well as a hallowed space where warriors could level up their abilities and manufacture their characters.

The introduction of Abdulmanap's child, Khabib, in 1988, added another aspect to his excursion. The connection among father and child would develop into an organization based on common regard, trust, and a common vision for significance. As Khabib moved into the universe of combative techniques, directed by the consistent hand of his dad, the Nurmagomedov heritage started to unfurl in the most unforeseen of fields — the worldwide phase of blended combative techniques.

Abdulmanap Nurmagomedov's initial life and childhood, implanted in the social mosaic of Dagestan, laid the preparation for a heritage that would rise above borders and resound with warriors and fans across the globe. His excursion, set apart by the upsides of difficult work, discipline, and an unfaltering obligation to greatness, turned into a demonstration of the unyielding soul of a Dagestani hero. As we dig further into the layers of Abdulmanap's story, we start to unwind the account of a mentor as well as the adventure of a visionary whose impact would leave a getting through engrave on the universe of combative techniques.

2. **Exploration of his passion for martial arts and the roots of his coaching philosophy.**

Abdulmanap Nurmagomedov's excursion into the universe of combative techniques was not only a quest for actual dominance; it was a profoundly imbued enthusiasm that would shape his character and make a permanent imprint on the scene of blended hand to hand fighting (MMA). To comprehend the man behind the mentor, one should disentangle the layers of Abdulmanap's initial experiences with the craft of battle and follow the underlying foundations of the instructing reasoning that would later characterize his heritage.

From his early stages in Dagestan, Abdulmanap showed a characteristic tendency towards proactive tasks. The rough scenes of his country gave a characteristic jungle gym to a young man anxious to test his grit. Wrestling, profoundly implanted in the social texture of Dagestan, turned into the principal field where Abdulmanap's enthusiasm for hand to hand fighting started to show.

The wrestling mats, where the conflict of bodies repeated like a cadenced dance, turned into a hallowed space for Abdulmanap. The customary Dagestani wrestling, known as Khapsagay, was not just a game but rather a social practice went down through ages.

It was in this antiquated discipline that Abdulmanap found the combination of rawness, technique, and the significant feeling of honor that characterized Dagestani hand to hand fighting.

As he drenched himself in the realm of wrestling, Abdulmanap tracked down comfort and reason in the restrained routine of preparing. The wrestling rec centers, frequently unobtrusive and honest, became safe-havens where the reverberations of strides and the snorts of effort were a demonstration of the devotion of the people who looked for dominance over their bodies. It was here, on the mats, that Abdulmanap's excursion into the core of hand to hand fighting genuinely started.

The Dagestani ethos, well established in the North Caucasus locale, imparted in Abdulmanap a feeling of obligation to maintain the honorable upsides, strength, and local area. Wrestling, as a microcosm of this bigger social embroidery, turned into a material on which Abdulmanap could communicate his obligation to these beliefs. The discipline expected in the wrestling field, both in preparing and contest, filled in as a cauldron that fashioned his personality.

Past the rawness of the game, wrestling in Dagestan conveyed an otherworldly aspect. It was not just about overwhelming an adversary; it was about the epitome of custom, the transmission of social insight, and the manufacturing of bonds that stretched out past the limits of the recreation center. This all encompassing comprehension of hand to hand fighting, where actual ability was entwined with social personality, laid the preparation for Abdulmanap's more extensive way of thinking as a mentor.

As Abdulmanap's capability in wrestling developed, so did his interest in different types of combative techniques. The world past Dagestan called, offering a different exhibit of disciplines ready to be investigated. Judo, with its accentuation on equilibrium and method, caught Abdulmanap's advantage. The quest for information turned into a main thrust, convincing him to wander past the recognizable bounds of his country.

His investigation of various combative techniques was not only a mission for specialized dominance; it was an excursion of self-disclosure and scholarly improvement. Each discipline turned into a part in the developing story of's how Abdulmanap might interpret battle sports. From the hooking strategies of wrestling to the tosses and entries of judo, he retained the complexities of every fine art, perceiving the interesting commitments they could make to his developing way of thinking.

Abdulmanap's enthusiasm for hand to hand fighting was not restricted to the actual parts of preparing. It included a profound appreciation for the psychological and otherworldly components of battle. The hand to hand fighting turned into a vehicle for personal development, a method through which one could develop discipline, flexibility, and a feeling of direction.

This comprehensive viewpoint established the groundwork for the instructing reasoning that would later become inseparable from Abdulmanap Nurmagomedov.

The convergence of hand to hand fighting and otherworldliness turned out to be especially articulated as Abdulmanap dug into the lessons of Islam. Dagestan, with its dominatingly Muslim populace, gave a social setting wherein the standards of the confidence were woven into the actual texture of day to day existence. Islam, with its accentuation on discipline, modesty, and the quest for greatness, resounded profoundly with Abdulmanap's own way of thinking.

The mosque, with its minarets coming to towards the sky, turned into a position of comfort and reflection for Abdulmanap. The standards embraced in Islamic lessons — regard for other people, the significance of local area, and the quest for information — tracked down reverberation in his way to deal with training. The gyms where he prepared warriors were not simply spaces for functional preparing; they were fields where the upsides of Islam were appeared through the discipline of hand to hand fighting.

Abdulmanap's training reasoning started to come to fruition as he amalgamated the different impacts that molded his excursion. The wrestling fields of Dagestan imparted in him a feeling of discipline, durability, and the significance of flexibility notwithstanding difficulty. The investigation of various combative techniques expanded his specialized collection, permitting him to draw upon a different arrangement of abilities while molding the warriors under his direction.

Fundamental to Abdulmanap's training reasoning was the confidence in the groundbreaking force of mentorship. The connection among mentor and competitor, he got it, stretched out past the limits of the rec center. It was an organization based on trust, common regard, and a common vision for progress. The mentorship model he embraced was not exclusively centered around actual preparation; it incorporated the comprehensive improvement of the person as a military craftsman and personally.

As Abdulmanap changed from being an expert of combative techniques to a mentor, the subtleties of his instructing reasoning turned out to be more clear. The gyms under his tutelage were not simply spaces for actual effort; they were research facilities for character improvement. Abdulmanap tried to impart in his contenders not simply the specialized abilities expected for progress in the enclosure yet in addition the ethics that would work well for them throughout everyday life.

Discipline, a foundation of Abdulmanap's childhood in Dagestan, was a focal fundamental of his training theory. He trusted that progress in hand to hand fighting, as throughout everyday life, was dependent upon the development of a trained brain and body.

The thorough preparation regimens, the redundancy of procedures, and the accentuation on mental courage were all parts of a more extensive system to saturate warriors with the flexibility expected to explore the difficulties of rivalry and then some.

Regard, one more key worth imbued in Abdulmanap's training theory, stretched out in different bearings. Contenders were instructed to regard their adversaries, their mentors, and themselves. The ethos of regard pervaded the rec center, establishing a climate where people from different foundations could meet up in quest for a shared objective. The illustrations of regard learned on the mats were planned to rise above the universe of combative techniques and penetrate the warriors' communications in the more extensive local area.

Lowliness was one more mainstay of Abdulmanap's training reasoning. He comprehended that the quest for dominance was a continuous excursion, and regardless of the honors or triumphs, modesty stayed an excellence to be treasured. Contenders were urged not to see a good outcome as an objective but rather as a consistent course of personal development. This approach cultivated a culture where self images were saved, and the emphasis stayed on the steady development of abilities and character.

Abdulmanap's training reasoning likewise stressed the significance of local area and the equal connection among contenders and the general public they addressed. The progress of a singular contender was viewed as an aggregate victory for the local area, and warriors were helped to remember the obligations that accompanied their situations as good examples. Abdulmanap accepted that hand to hand fighting could act as an impetus for positive change, inside the bounds of the rec center as well as in the more extensive social texture.

The underlying foundations of Abdulmanap Nurmagomedov's training reasoning, profoundly implanted in the dirt of Dagestan's military practices, were supported by an energy for hand to hand fighting that rose above the actual parts of battle. His excursion from the wrestling mats of his country to the worldwide phase of MMA was set apart by a ceaseless course of learning, transformation, and a pledge to the rules that characterized his personality.

As he remained toward the side of the octagon, directing his child Khabib and different warriors to triumph, Abdulmanap's training reasoning was not only a bunch of standards scratched on paper; it was a no nonsense ethos that energized the spirits of those under his tutelage. The investigation of his energy for combative techniques and the foundations of his training reasoning uncovers the development of a mentor as well as the unfurling of a significant vision — one that rises above the limits of game and leaves a getting through heritage in the hearts and brains of warriors and fans the same.

3. Initial experiences in training and shaping aspiring fighters.

Abdulmanap Nurmagomedov's excursion from an energetic military craftsman to a venerated mentor was set apart by a progression of extraordinary encounters, each adding to the development of his instructing reasoning. As he progressed into the job of a guide, Abdulmanap's initial encounters in preparing and molding hopeful contenders assumed a urgent part in forming the underpinning of his training inheritance.

In the recreation centers of Dagestan, where Abdulmanap's own excursion into combative techniques had unfurled, he made his underlying strides as a mentor. The change from a professional to a guide denoted a change in outlook in his relationship with the universe of battle sports. The wrestling mats, when a space for self-improvement, presently turned into the material on which he painted the goals of another age of contenders.

The gym, with its powerful mix of sweat-splashed assurance and the indisputable fragrance of discipline, turned into a cauldron where Abdulmanap's instructing reasoning started to take substantial structure. His initial encounters in training were not just about conferring specialized abilities; they were tied in with imparting an outlook — an ethos that would characterize the contenders under his direction.

Abdulmanap's training debut matched with an expanding interest in blended hand to hand fighting (MMA), a game that would come to characterize the Nurmagomedov name on the worldwide stage. MMA, with its combination of different disciplines, introduced the two open doors and difficulties for a mentor saturated with the customs of wrestling and other hand to hand fighting. It was a domain where flexibility and a nuanced comprehension of different battling styles became fundamental.

The principal partner of warriors under Abdulmanap's direction was a different gathering, mirroring the cosmopolitan idea of Dagestan's military scene. Warriors with foundations in wrestling, judo, and striking disciplines united in the exercise center, each bringing their exceptional ranges of abilities and goals. Abdulmanap's job was to incorporate this variety into a strong unit, where the qualities of every contender supplemented the shortcomings of others.

In these underlying instructional meetings, Abdulmanap accentuated the basics — striking, catching, and entries. The goal was not to shape duplicates of a particular battling style however to make balanced military craftsmen equipped for adjusting to different situations in the flighty scene of MMA. His training reasoning, established in a comprehensive way to deal with battle, was clear as he looked to construct contenders who were flexible, key, and restrained.

Discipline, a worth imbued in Abdulmanap's childhood, was a non-debatable component of his training theory. Warriors were supposed to stick to a thorough preparation routine, showing up reliably and giving their maximum effort in each meeting. The rec center, under Abdulmanap's careful focus, turned into a space where reasons were saved, and obligation to progress was principal.

Notwithstanding actual discipline, Abdulmanap granted mental discipline to his warriors. The mental parts of battle, frequently neglected by certain mentors, were fundamental to Abdulmanap's methodology. Representation, mental grit, and the capacity to remain created under tension were stressed as fundamental parts of a warrior's tool stash. This comprehensive point of view repeated the Dagestani conviction that hand to hand fighting was about actual ability as well as about the development of a solid psyche and unyielding soul.

The fellowship among contenders, cultivated by Abdulmanap's instructing reasoning, made a feeling of local area inside the rec center. The variety of foundations and ranges of abilities among the warriors turned into a wellspring of solidarity as opposed to division.

Abdulmanap energized a culture where experienced warriors guided the novices, cultivating a climate of shared information and common help.

As the warriors advanced in their preparation, Abdulmanap acquainted an essential aspect with their turn of events. Battle planning was not only a question of practical preparation; it was a careful course of concentrating on rivals, recognizing shortcomings, and formulating blueprints custom fitted to every individual contender. Abdulmanap's logical way to deal with battles exhibited his profound comprehension of the chess-like intricacies intrinsic in MMA.

The recreation centers where Abdulmanap directed his instructing meetings were not simply puts for actual effort; they were labs for character improvement. Regard, one more guiding principle of his instructing reasoning, saturated each cooperation inside the rec center. Contenders were instructed to regard their mentors, preparing accomplices, and the actual game. The order inside the rec center was not tyrant yet in light of gained appreciation, establishing a climate where trust thrived.

The mentorship model that Abdulmanap embraced was substantial in his relationship with every contender. The connection among mentor and competitor went past the specialized parts of preparing. Abdulmanap served not just as an aide in that frame of mind of combative techniques yet additionally as a guide in the more extensive excursion of life. The exercise center turned into a space where contenders leveled up their abilities as well as consumed the insight and values conferred by their mentor.

The meaning of Abdulmanap's training reasoning was maybe most obvious in the advancement of his own child, Khabib Nurmagomedov. Khabib, who might proceed to become one of the most predominant warriors in MMA history, was not only a result of his dad's hereditary genealogy; he was a demonstration of the viability of Abdulmanap's training standards.

The connection among Abdulmanap and Khabib rose above the normal mentor competitor dynamic. It was a dad child organization based on common regard, trust, and a common vision for significance. Abdulmanap's training of Khabib was not tied in with making a hero for the world; it was tied in with sustaining a young fellow to live up to his true capacity and encapsulate the qualities imparted in him since early on.

The early encounters in preparing and molding hopeful contenders under Abdulmanap's direction laid the foundation for the achievement that would follow. As his contenders contended in provincial and public contests, the adequacy of his training reasoning turned out to be progressively obvious. The standards of discipline, regard, mental strength, and versatility were not simply hypothetical ideas; they were the core values that pushed his contenders to triumph.

Abdulmanap's training inheritance kept on developing as the progress of his contenders gathered consideration past the lines of Dagestan. The Nurmagomedov name became inseparable from greatness in MMA, a demonstration of the training reasoning that had been developed in the exercise rooms of a district known for its hero soul. Contenders from different regions of the planet tried to prepare under Abdulmanap, drawn by the specialized mastery as well as by the groundbreaking ethos that characterized his instructing.

The development of Abdulmanap Nurmagomedov as a mentor was not a direct movement; it was a nonstop course of learning, transformation, and refinement. The exercise rooms of Dagestan, where he initially started his training process, turned into the cauldron where his way of thinking was verified compelling. The tradition of his initial encounters in preparing and forming hopeful warriors stays in the triumphs of his proteges as well as in the getting through influence on the ethos of MMA and the existences of those he contacted.

Chapter 1

The Nurmagomedov Dynasty

The Nurmagomedov Tradition, a celebrated heredity well established in the rough territory of Dagestan, remains as a demonstration of the unyielding soul and military ability that rises above ages. At its rudder, the patriarch Abdulmanap Nurmagomedov, a man whose vision and responsibility fashioned an inheritance that has made a permanent imprint on the universe of blended hand to hand fighting (MMA).

Abdulmanap, brought into the world in 1962 in the precipitous locale of Sildi in Dagestan, was no more abnormal to misfortune. Experiencing childhood in a climate that requested strength, he floated towards battle sports quite early on. The cruel scenes of Dagestan, with its rich wrestling custom, gave the ideal scenery to Abdulmanap to develop his enthusiasm for hard to hand fighting.

In the beginning phases of his excursion, Abdulmanap dove into different trains like wrestling, judo, and sambo, each adding to the mixed mix of abilities that would later characterize his instructing reasoning. His encounters formed his way to deal with the game as well as imparted in him a significant comprehension of the extraordinary force of discipline and difficult work.

Abdulmanap's command as a mentor started when he expected administration at the Hawks MMA Club in Dagestan, a preparation ground that would proceed to deliver probably the most impressive contenders on the planet. It was here that the underpinning of the Nurmagomedov Tradition was laid, where Abdulmanap's instructing standards turned into the foundation of an imposing genealogy.

One of the most famous figures to rise out of this line is Abdulmanap's own child, Khabib Nurmagomedov. Brought into the world in 1988, Khabib retained the lessons of his dad from a young age. The dad child couple produced a bond that reached out past familial ties; it turned into the bedrock of Khabib's unrivaled progress in the MMA field. Under Abdulmanap's direction, Khabib turned into a talented warrior as well as encapsulated the upsides of discipline, regard, and lowliness imparted by his dad.

Khabib's excursion to UFC fame is inseparable from the ascent of the Nurmagomedov Administration. Undefeated in his expert vocation, Khabib's predominance in the lightweight division exhibited the climax of long stretches of fastidious preparation and an outlook formed by the lessons of Abdulmanap. The picture of Khabib getting many triumphs, finishing in his close to home goodbye at UFC 254, resounded as a singular victory as well as the victory of a heritage based on penance and resolute assurance.

Unfortunately, Abdulmanap's life was stopped in 2020, leaving a void in the Nurmagomedov Line. The misfortune resonated inside the family as well as across the whole MMA people group. Nonetheless, Abdulmanap's inheritance persevered, conveyed forward by Khabib and the warriors who keep on preparing under the standard of the Birds MMA Club.

The quintessence of the Nurmagomedov Administration lies in triumphs inside the octagon as well as in the qualities it gives. Abdulmanap's lessons reached out past the domain of combative techniques; they embodied a lifestyle, a way of thinking that underscored the improvement of character close by athletic ability. The Warriors arising out of the Nurmagomedov stable weren't simply gifted soldiers; they were people produced in the pot of discipline, regard, and strength.

As Khabib pulled back from the game, the inquiry waited: What next for the Nurmagomedov Line? The response appeared as the future. While Khabib formally resigned, the heritage lives on through his family members and proteges who keep on leading. Umar Nurmagomedov, Khabib's cousin, arose as a promising contender, meaning the propagation of the family's military custom.

Past the cutthroat field, the Nurmagomedov Line's impact stretched out into the more extensive social scene. Dagestan, when a locale eclipsed by international intricacies, became inseparable from military greatness. The Birds MMA Club turned into an image of expectation and desire for youthful contenders, repeating Abdulmanap's conviction that through discipline and difficult work, one could conquer any deterrent.

The Nurmagomedov Tradition remains as a living demonstration of the groundbreaking force of combative techniques. Abdulmanap Nurmagomedov's vision, imparted in the hearts and brains of his replacements, keeps on molding warriors as well as people who convey forward a heritage based on discipline, regard, and unflinching responsibility. As the excursion of the Nurmagomedov Line unfurls, it is in excess of a story of triumphs; it is an account of versatility, family, and the persevering through soul that characterizes the pith of combative techniques.

1.1 Overview of the Nurmagomedov family's rich martial arts history.

The Nurmagomedov family's combative techniques history is an embroidery woven with strings of discipline, strength, and a resolute obligation to the specialty. Established in the tough scenes of Dagestan, a locale known for its celebrated wrestling custom, the Nurmagomedovs have cut a specialty for themselves in the chronicles of blended combative techniques (MMA). In charge of this celebrated family stands Abdulmanap Nurmagomedov, a patriarch whose vision and devotion have molded a heritage that reaches out a long ways past the limits of the octagon.

Abdulmanap, brought into the world in 1962 in the town of Sildi, Dagestan, was acquainted with the universe of battle sports since the beginning. The unforgiving yet supporting climate of Dagestan gave a prolific ground to the development of his energy. Wrestling, judo, and sambo became quests for actual ability as well as roads through which Abdulmanap sharpened his personality and hard working attitude. The rough scenes reflected the versatility that would come to characterize the Nurmagomedov family's way to deal with hand to hand fighting.

As Abdulmanap's process unfurled, he arose not similarly as a talented expert of different military teaches however as a visionary mentor. In the mid 2000s, he assumed control over the Falcons MMA Club in Dagestan, an essential second that would shape the direction of the Nurmagomedov family's combative techniques inheritance. The club turned into a pot where warriors were not simply prepared in strategy but rather shaped into people of unflinching discipline and mental strength.

The most noticeable figure to rise out of this familial cauldron is Abdulmanap's child, Khabib Nurmagomedov. Brought into the world in 1988, Khabib retained the ethos of hand to hand fighting from his dad, soaking up the methods as well as the qualities that would later characterize his way to deal with the game. Khabib's excursion from the nearby Dagestani circuits to worldwide fame in the UFC typifies the climax of long periods of restrained preparing and the dauntless soul imparted by his dad.

The Nurmagomedov family's combative techniques heritage is a demonstration of the exchange of nature and support. While Dagestan's rich wrestling legacy gave a fruitful ground to the family's military interests, it was Abdulmanap's vision that raised their undertakings higher than ever.

The Hawks MMA Club, under his administration, turned into a mixture of ability and assurance, creating contenders who vanquished rivals in the enclosure as well as typified the ethos of combative techniques in their day to day routines.

The foundation of the Nurmagomedov family's combative techniques reasoning is discipline. Abdulmanap, a steadfast devotee to the groundbreaking force of discipline, ingrained this uprightness as the bedrock of his training. Instructional courses at the Hawks MMA Club were thorough, requesting actual effort as well as a psychological versatility that put his contenders aside. It wasn't just about winning sessions; it was tied in with becoming people of substance, character, and faithful purpose.

The tradition of the Nurmagomedov family reaches out past the octagon, pervading the social texture of Dagestan. The family turned into a wellspring of motivation for hopeful warriors in the locale, turning the focus on Dagestan as a hotbed of military ability. Adolescents, captivated by the progress of Khabib and his peers, rushed to the Birds MMA Club, to gain proficiency with the procedures of battle as well as to ingest the qualities that made the Nurmagomedovs paragons of the game.

Misfortune struck the Nurmagomedov family in 2020 when Abdulmanap, the patriarch and directing power, died. His end left a void inside the family as well as inside the whole MMA people group. The generous flood of sympathies and accolades from contenders, mentors, and fans overall highlighted the significant effect Abdulmanap had on the game. Be that as it may, as the proverb goes, the show should go on, and the Nurmagomedov family, however grieving, kept on leading.

Khabib, having made unrivaled progress in the UFC, reported his retirement around the same time as his dad's elapsing. The choice denoted the conclusion of a significant time period in numerous ways, however it likewise opened another section for the Nurmagomedov family. The inquiry waited: What next for the family's combative techniques inheritance?

The response unfurled through the development of the future. Umar Nurmagomedov, Khabib's cousin, ventured into the spotlight, conveying forward the family's military practice. Umar, as Khabib, displayed a mix of specialized ability and mental strength that indicated a progression of the Nurmagomedov inheritance. As he entered the MMA scene, Umar conveyed the heaviness of assumptions as a warrior as well as a torchbearer for the family's military legacy.

The Nurmagomedov family's hand to hand fighting history isn't bound to individual accomplishments; it exemplifies a more extensive story of social effect. Dagestan, when eclipsed by international intricacies, arose as a guide of military greatness. The Hawks MMA Club turned into an image of trust, a demonstration of what discipline, difficult work, and immovable responsibility could accomplish.

The Nurmagomedovs, through their excursion, reclassified discernments about the district, demonstrating that significance could rise out of the most improbable of spots.

The Nurmagomedov family's combative techniques history is an adventure of wins, hardships, and a guarantee to greatness. From the modest starting points in Dagestan to worldwide acknowledgment in the UFC, the family's process is a demonstration of the extraordinary force of hand to hand fighting. Abdulmanap Nurmagomedov, as the designer of this inheritance, made a permanent imprint on his family as well as on the actual game. As the Nurmagomedov story keeps on unfurling, it represents more than triumphs in the enclosure; it addresses the getting through soul of a family limited by the quest for military greatness and the qualities that make champions both inside and outside the ring.

1.2 Abdulmanap's role in preserving and advancing the family legacy.

Abdulmanap Nurmagomedov, the patriarch of the celebrated Nurmagomedov family, assumed an instrumental part in safeguarding and propelling a hand to hand fighting heritage that rises above ages. Brought into the world in 1962 in the rough territory of Sildi, Dagestan, Abdulmanap's process started against the setting of a district saturated with wrestling custom. His initial openness to the universe of battle sports established the groundwork for a long lasting obligation to combative techniques, a responsibility that would proceed to shape the predetermination of the Nurmagomedov family.

Abdulmanap's initial years were set apart by the brutal real factors of life in Dagestan, a district known for its rough scenes and a versatile populace. It was in the midst of this difficult climate that Abdulmanap's partiality for battle sports bloomed. Wrestling, judo, and sambo became athletic pursuits as well as roads through which he explored the intricacies of life. The qualities imparted by these disciplines — discipline, versatility, and regard — would turn into the core values of Abdulmanap's instructing reasoning.

As Abdulmanap developed, so did how he might interpret the groundbreaking force of combative techniques. In the mid 2000s, he expected initiative at the Falcons MMA Club in Dagestan, a critical crossroads that undeniable the formalization of the Nurmagomedov family's hand to hand fighting inheritance. The club turned into a pot where Abdulmanap's vision came to fruition — a dream that reached out past the development of gifted warriors to the improvement of people whose character reflected the unyielding soul of Dagestan.

Abdulmanap's instructing theory was portrayed by a comprehensive methodology that rose above simple specialized capability. While the warriors under his tutelage positively improved their abilities, they likewise went through a transformation in character. The Falcons MMA Club turned into a research facility where discipline was not simply a preparation necessity but rather a lifestyle.

Abdulmanap comprehended that genuine significance in combative techniques wasn't bound to triumphs in the enclosure yet was reflected in the manner in which his warriors behaved beyond it.

The apex of Abdulmanap's training profession appeared through his relationship with his child, Khabib Nurmagomedov. From the beginning of's first experience with wrestling in their home to the fabulous phases of the UFC, the dad child pair exemplified the harmonious connection among coach and follower. Abdulmanap's impact on Khabib wasn't simply specialized; it was significant in its capacity to shape the mentality of a future UFC champion.

Under Abdulmanap's direction, Khabib turned out to be something other than a contender; he turned into a leading figure for the Nurmagomedov inheritance. Undefeated in his expert profession, Khabib's strength in the UFC's lightweight division was a confirmation not exclusively to his expertise however to the standards imparted by his dad. The world saw a warrior who, past the craft of battle, exemplified discipline, regard, and modesty — the actual pith of Abdulmanap's lessons.

Abdulmanap's job in safeguarding and propelling the family heritage stretched out a long ways past the limits of instructional courses and the octagon. He turned into a coach to his organic kids as well as to a more extensive local area of warriors who looked for his direction. His insight, frequently conveyed as illustrations and tales, resounded with a well known fact that rose above social and etymological limits. Warriors from different foundations ran to the Hawks MMA Club, to learn strategies as well as to retain the ethos of a that military man expressions was an excursion of self-revelation however much it was a way to triumph.

The Nurmagomedov family's hand to hand fighting heritage confronted a significant test in 2020 when Abdulmanap, the planner of this line, died. His demise sent shockwaves through the MMA world, leaving a void that appeared to be difficult. In any case, the very standards he granted to his family and warriors — flexibility and steadiness — turned into the directing lights that enlightened the way ahead.

Following Abdulmanap's passing, the inquiry emerged: Might the Nurmagomedov family and the Birds MMA Club at any point keep on flourishing without its visionary chief? The response unfurled through the activities of those he had affected. Khabib, notwithstanding the profound cost, kept on supporting the family heritage in different limits. The Hawks MMA Club, however grieving, arose as a demonstration of the getting through effect of Abdulmanap's lessons. Warriors kept on preparing, rivalries were challenged, and triumphs were accomplished, all in the soul of respecting the heritage that Abdulmanap had constructed.

The Nurmagomedov family inheritance entered another stage as Khabib formally resigned from proficient rivalry. The void left by his takeoff was unmistakable, however it likewise flagged a change in center toward the future.

Umar Nurmagomedov, Khabib's cousin, ventured into the spotlight, conveying forward the family's military practices. Umar's development reflected a familial commitment as well as a certifiable obligation to the standards instilled by Abdulmanap.

Umar, as Khabib before him, turned into a torchbearer for the Nurmagomedov heritage. As he entered the universe of expert MMA, the examinations with Khabib were inescapable, yet Umar exhibited his special mix of abilities and mental strength. The Nurmagomedov family's combative techniques venture proceeded, presently with another hero who conveyed the heaviness of assumptions yet in addition the insight acquired from the people who preceded him.

The Nurmagomedov family's hand to hand fighting inheritance isn't only an account of triumphs and losses; a story rises above the game. Abdulmanap's job in safeguarding and propelling this heritage was likened to that of a social overseer. Through combative techniques, he raised his family as well as a whole locale — Dagestan — onto the worldwide stage. The Hawks MMA Club turned into an image of yearning, demonstrating that significance could rise out of the most impossible of spots.

Abdulmanap Nurmagomedov's job in protecting and propelling the family heritage was one of significant importance. He wasn't simply a mentor; he was a wise whose lessons rose above the domains of game to contact the actual substance of human person. The Nurmagomedov family's hand to hand fighting excursion, however set apart by wins and hardships, remains as a demonstration of the getting through force of discipline, flexibility, and steady responsibility. Abdulmanap's heritage lives on in the triumphs of his family as well as in the hearts and brains of the people who keep on being motivated by the standards he advocated all through his surprising life.

1.3 Anecdotes and stories showcasing the familial bonds and dedication to martial arts.

The Nurmagomedov family's excursion in the domain of hand to hand fighting isn't simply a narrative of triumphs and procedures; it is a rich embroidery woven with tales and stories that enlighten the familial bonds and relentless commitment to the specialty. At the core of these stories is Abdulmanap Nurmagomedov, the patriarch whose vision and responsibility set up for a heritage that rises above the limits of the octagon.

One powerful account beholds back to Abdulmanap's initial a long time in Dagestan, where the Nurmagomedov family's association with hand to hand fighting was first manufactured. As a little fellow experiencing childhood in the town of Sildi, Abdulmanap ended up attracted to the nearby wrestling society. Dagestan, with its soaks history in catching and battle sports, turned into a fruitful ground for the Nurmagomedov family's military interests.

First experience with wrestling wasn't through proper preparation in an exercise center yet rather through the day to day customs of life in Dagestan. Wrestling wasn't simply a game; it was an approach to holding, a language verbally expressed locally. Fathers bestowed the craftsmanship to their children, uncles imparted methods to nephews, and the actual town turned into a living preparation ground. These early encounters established the groundwork for a familial bond produced in the pot of rawness and shared energy.

The familial bonds inside the Nurmagomedov family are maybe best exemplified in the connection among Abdulmanap and his child, Khabib. Stories from their common process portray a dad not only instructing his child however of a coach molding the outlook of a future hero. In the peaceful corners of their home, the reverberations of wrestling matches resonated as Abdulmanap bestowed specialized information as well as the elusive characteristics that characterize a genuine military craftsman — discipline, regard, and a steady hard working attitude.

One especially loved story spins around the offhand instructional courses that occurred in the Nurmagomedov family. Abdulmanap, perceiving the expected in his child since early on, would draw in Khabib in wrestling matches solidly in their lounge. The homegrown setting changed into a field where the underpinnings of Khabib's hooking ability were laid. It wasn't just about learning moves; it was tied in with retaining the quintessence of the game through the cozy trade among father and child.

As Khabib's advantage in combative techniques extended, Abdulmanap's obligation to his child's improvement turned out to be progressively obvious. The family's lounge matches advanced into more conventional preparation, with Abdulmanap acquainting Khabib with the more extensive universe of battle sports. The familial connection between them turned into a wellspring of solidarity, a relationship that wasn't simply characterized by blood however by a common enthusiasm for military greatness.

The Nurmagomedov family's devotion to combative techniques is likewise highlighted by the foundation and advancement of the Hawks MMA Club in Dagestan. As Abdulmanap expected initiative of the club, it turned into a point of convergence for the family as well as for a local area of contenders trying to improve their abilities under his direction. The exercise center wasn't just a preparation office; it was a collective space where the familial ethos stretched out past direct relations.

One piercing story exudes from the walls of the Falcons MMA Club, where warriors from different foundations saw as a usual hangout spot. Abdulmanap's instructing rose above the details of battle; it turned into an all encompassing methodology that addressed the psychological, profound, and, surprisingly, otherworldly components of hand to hand fighting. Contenders prepared under a mentor as well as inside a family, where the bonds produced in the pot of preparing stretched out to kinship outside the rec center.

The familial bonds inside the Birds MMA Club were clear not just in that frame of mind among Abdulmanap and the warriors yet additionally among the actual contenders. Instructional meetings were set apart by a feeling of fraternity, a common quest for greatness that reflected the familial qualities imparted by Abdulmanap. Stories proliferate of warriors supporting each other through triumphs and losses, typifying the aggregate soul of the Nurmagomedov family's commitment to hand to hand fighting.

The story of Khabib's ascent to worldwide conspicuousness in the UFC fills in as a demonstration of the familial bonds that energized his excursion. One especially piercing second happened during Khabib's UFC debut in 2012. Abdulmanap, unfit to be available face to face because of visa issues, watched his child's battle from Dagestan. The distance, be that as it may, didn't reduce the familial association. In the consequence of Khabib's triumph, the profound call among father and child caught the embodiment of their common victory.

Abdulmanap's words, verbally expressed from a far distance, were not only those of a mentor; they were the opinions of a saw his child's dad rising to a worldwide stage. The familial connection between them, built up through long stretches of shared penance and commitment to combative techniques, rose above actual distances. It was a second that highlighted the interconnectedness of their excursions, an association of ages limited by a common enthusiasm for the art.

The Nurmagomedov family's devotion to combative techniques stretches out past the octagon into the more extensive social scene of Dagestan. Tales from the locale discuss the family's job in rousing another age of contenders. Adolescents experiencing childhood in the tough towns of Dagestan found in the Nurmagomedovs sports symbols as well as images of probability. The familial bonds inside the Nur-magomedov family turned into a wellspring of motivation for trying contenders, an update that significance could be accomplished through discipline and commitment.

One especially resounding story rises out of a visit by Khabib to a neighborhood school in Dagestan. Seeing youngsters, wide-looked at and anxious, paying attention to Khabib's words said a lot about the family's effect on the local area. The familial ethos of the Nurmagomedovs, where combative techniques were a quest for individual brilliance as well as a way of discipline and ideals, turned into a directing light for the future.

The commitment to hand to hand fighting inside the Nurmagomedov family is maybe most obvious in the lessons and anecdotes shared by Abdulmanap. His words, frequently conveyed in a way that mixed insight with straightforwardness, turned into the ethical compass for warriors under his tutelage. Stories from instructional courses and confidential discussions portray a man who comprehended that hand to hand fighting was in excess of an actual undertaking; it was an excursion of self-revelation and self-awareness.

One such account rotates around Abdulmanap's accentuation on discipline. He would frequently describe stories from his own life, where discipline turned into the way to conquering difficulties. The illustration wasn't simply hypothetical; it was a lived experience shared inside the familial setting of the Falcons MMA Club. Contenders, whether hopeful beginners or old pros, retained these lessons as guidelines for preparing as well as standards for living.

The familial bonds inside the Nurmagomedov family took on an impactful aspect during Khabib's title session at UFC 254. Abdulmanap, fighting medical problems, couldn't be genuinely present, yet his soul posed a potential threat over the occasion. In a representative signal, Khabib left his gloves in the focal point of the octagon, a recognition for his dad and coach. The familial association, manufactured through long periods of shared penance, commitment, and love for combative techniques, tracked down articulation in that serious second.

The tales and stories from the Nurmagomedov family's excursion in hand to hand fighting are not only accounts of wins; they are impressions of the qualities that characterize the quintessence of the game. The familial connections between ages, the devotion to an art that goes past the quest for titles, and the effect on a local area resound as persevering through subjects. The Nurmagomedov family, through its accounts, has carved an inheritance that rises above the limits of the octagon, turning into a wellspring of motivation for warriors, families, and networks around the world.

The Nurmagomedov family's devotion to hand to hand fighting is additionally exemplified from the perspective of shared penance. Stories proliferate with respect to the strenuous idea of instructional courses and the familial help that supported them. As Khabib sought after greatness in the UFC, Abdulmanap's job as both mentor and father turned out to be progressively articulated. The family's obligation to the game wasn't restricted to the spotlight of fields yet reached out into the less apparent domains of day to day existence.

One strong account unfurls during the instructional courses paving the way to Khabib's high-stakes battles. Abdulmanap, perceptive of the actual cost for his child, would frequently join Khabib in the tiring meetings. Father and child, limited by a pledge to combative techniques, would stretch each other to the edges of physical and mental perseverance. The familial bonds reinforced through shared sweat and effort, a demonstration of the profundity of their devotion to the art.

The Nurmagomedov family's devotion to hand to hand fighting additionally appeared in their aggregate reaction to mishaps. Wounds, routs, and the unavoidable difficulties of a contender's process were met not with discouragement but rather with flexibility. Abdulmanap, drawing from his own encounters, granted the insight that mishaps were not road obstructions but rather potential open doors for development. The familial encouraging group of people turned into a wellspring of solidarity during these testing times, supporting that genuine heroes are characterized by triumphs as well as by their capacity to ascend after a fall.

The Nurmagomedov family's association with hand to hand fighting isn't exclusively restricted to the male individuals. Tales from the family's story feature the job of Khabib's sister, Amina, who, while not an expert contender, assumed a critical part in supporting her sibling's process. Her attendance at battles and her relentless consolation highlighted the comprehensive idea of the family's commitment to hand to hand fighting. The familial bonds reached out past orientation standards, embracing an aggregate obligation to the standards supported by Abdulmanap.

The meaning of family inside the Nurmagomedov account is additionally highlighted through social practices. Dagestan, with its rich woven artwork of customs and ceremonies, turned into a basic piece of the family's excursion. Tales from festivities, where the triumphs of one relative became shared wins, grandstand the indivisible connection between the Nurmagomedovs' devotion to combative techniques and their social roots.

Abdulmanap's job as a social caretaker is obvious in the narratives of how he integrated Dagestani customs into the texture of the Falcons MMA Club. The rec center wasn't simply a space for actual preparation; it was a social center where contenders soaked up the upsides of their legacy. From the customary Dagestani dance, the lezginka, performed before battles to the shared dinners that reflected the glow of family social occasions, the Nurmagomedov family's commitment to combative techniques turned into a festival of their social character.

The Nurmagomedov family's process is additionally interspersed by cases of fellowship and mentorship inside the Birds MMA Club. Contenders from different foundations, attracted to the club's standing, found themselves leveling up their abilities as well as turning out to be important for a more distant family. The familial bonds manufactured inside the exercise center became apparent during instructional courses, where warriors upheld each other through the afflictions of arrangement.

One specific story describes a snapshot of weakness inside the Hawks MMA Club. In the midst of the actual requests of preparing, Abdulmanap cultivated a climate where contenders felt happy with communicating their feelings of dread and questions. The familial ethos rose above the customary mentor contender relationship, making a space where psychological wellness and profound prosperity were recognized and tended to. This supporting climate, initiated by Abdulmanap, highlighted the family's commitment to combative techniques as a comprehensive excursion including brain, body, and soul.

The Nurmagomedov family's devotion to hand to hand fighting stretches out into humanitarian undertakings, exhibiting a promise to local area past the bounds of the rec center. Tales from magnanimous drives led by Khabib and the family feature the conviction that combative techniques isn't simply a special goal yet a vehicle for positive social effect. The familial securities, manufactured through long periods of devotion to the art, presently stretch out to elevating the more extensive local area.

One especially moving story rotates around the development of a mosque to pay tribute to Abdulmanap Nurmagomedov in his local town of Sildi. The task, started by Khabib and upheld by the family, encapsulates the combination of the family's devotion to combative techniques with a more extensive obligation to local area and otherworldliness. The mosque fills in as an image of the getting through tradition of the Nurmagomedov family, rising above the domain of sports to add to the social and social texture of Dagestan.

The Nurmagomedov family's devotion to combative techniques is definitely not a static account; it is a living, developing story that keeps on unfurling. As Umar Nurmagomedov ventures into the spotlight, the familial bonds and obligation to the specialty persevere. Umar's excursion, similar as Khabib's before him, addresses a consistent coherence in the Nurmagomedov family's commitment to hand to hand fighting.

The familial ethos, molded by Abdulmanap's lessons, stays a directing power for the future.

The tales and stories inside the Nurmagomedov family's hand to hand fighting excursion uncover a story of familial bonds, shared penance, and a resolute devotion to the art. From the lounge matches that established the groundwork for Khabib's catching ability to the foundation of the Birds MMA Club as a shared space for contenders, the familial ethos has been the bedrock of their excursion. The tales radiating from Dagestan, the UFC fields, and the beneficent drives by and large paint a representation of a family whose devotion to combative techniques stretches out past individual accomplishments, embracing the more extensive domains of culture, local area, and positive effect. The Nurmagomedov family's story isn't just about triumphs; it is a story of versatility, social pride, and a promise to leaving an enduring inheritance that rises above the limits of the octagon.

Chapter 2

Crafting Champions

Making champions is a masterfulness that goes past the bounds of the actual field; it is a nuanced cycle that includes molding gifted competitors as well as people of character, flexibility, and unfaltering discipline. The story of making champions is distinctively typified in the excursion of the Nurmagomedov family, especially from the perspective of Abdulmanap Nurmagomedov, whose training reasoning rises above conventional thoughts of outcome in sports. This story unfurls against the setting of Dagestan, a district known for its rough scenes and rich wrestling custom, where the Nurmagomedov family's commitment to combative techniques has become inseparable from the specialty of making champions.

Abdulmanap Nurmagomedov, brought into the world in 1962 in the town of Sildi, Dagestan, was bound to turn into a critical designer in the family's tradition of making champions. His initial openness to battle sports in the brutal however supporting climate of Dagestan laid the preparation for a training reasoning that goes past specialized capability. Abdulmanap's process wasn't just about excelling at wrestling, judo, and sambo; it was tied in with figuring out the extraordinary force of discipline, mental guts, and the unstoppable soul expected to be a hero.

The embodiment of creating champions inside the Nurmagomedov family is best caught through the foundation of the Hawks MMA Club in Dagestan. The club, under Abdulmanap's initiative, turned into a cauldron where hopeful contenders were not only shown procedures but rather were etched into people of substance. The most common way of making champions, in this unique circumstance, wasn't bound to the actual preparation however reached out to the improvement of a mentality that could face the hardships of contest and life.

One essential part of Abdulmanap's training reasoning in making champions is the accentuation on discipline. The instructional meetings at the Falcons MMA Club were prestigious for their thoroughness, requesting actual effort as well as a psychological strength that put his contenders aside. Discipline wasn't only a prerequisite for progress in the enclosure; it was a lifestyle. Abdulmanap comprehended that creating champions included forming people who could explore difficulties with beauty and assurance.

The familial bonds inside the Nurmagomedov family assumed an essential part during the time spent making champions. The connection among Abdulmanap and his child, Khabib Nurmagomedov, exemplified the harmonious idea of mentorship and supporter. Khabib, brought into the world in 1988, turned into the living epitome of Abdulmanap's training reasoning. The familial association went past direct relations; it was a common excursion of penance, commitment, and the quest for greatness in the specialty of making champions.

Tales from Khabib's early stages feature the private idea of the familial bonds during the time spent creating champions. The lounge matches, where father and child participated in unrehearsed wrestling meetings, weren't just about actual preparation; they were snapshots of shared energy and an extending association with the game. The familial ethos turned into a wellspring of solidarity, establishing Khabib in the standards imparted by Abdulmanap as he explored the mind boggling scene of expert MMA.

The account of making champions additionally uncovers itself in the obligation to ceaseless advancing inside the Nurmagomedov family. Abdulmanap's instructing reasoning wasn't stale; it developed with the elements of the game and the exceptional traits of every warrior. The family's devotion to hand to hand fighting schooling stretched out past the walls of the Birds MMA Club, integrating bits of knowledge from different disciplines to advance the most common way of creating champions.

One part of making champions that separates the Nurmagomedov family is the social reconciliation inside their instructing reasoning. Dagestan's rich social legacy turned into a vital piece of the interaction. The conventional Dagestani dance, the lezginka, performed before battles, wasn't simply a custom; it was a festival of social pride and an exemplification of the familial bonds that characterize the specialty of making champions inside the Nurmagomedov heritage.

The Nurmagomedov family's devotion to combative techniques is additionally obvious in their capacity to explore difficulty as a basic piece of making champions. The game of MMA, known for its physical and mental difficulties, requires an interesting arrangement of abilities to change competitors into champions. Abdulmanap's lessons stretched out past specialized capability; they enveloped a mentality that embraced difficulty as a chance for development and refinement.

One of the extremely important occasions in the account of making champions came in the fallout of Khabib's loss to Gleison Tibau in 2012. The misfortune was an essential crossroads that tried Khabib's strength as well as the familial bonds inside the Nurmagomedov family. Abdulmanap's reaction to the difficulty was a masterclass in training reasoning. Rather than harping on the loss, he saw it as a pivotal opportunity for growth, a venturing stone on the way to turning into a genuine boss.

The account of creating champions arrived at its apex with Khabib's phenomenal undefeated disagreement the UFC. The summit of long stretches of commitment, discipline, and familial help worked out as expected as Khabib overwhelmed the lightweight division. His triumphs weren't simply individual victories; they were an aggregate demonstration of the specialty of creating champions inside the Nurmagomedov family. The familial bonds, formed through long stretches of shared penances, turned into the bedrock of Khabib's prosperity.

The idea of making champions inside the Nurmagomedov family reaches out past individual accomplishments to include the more extensive effect on the local area. Dagestan, when eclipsed by international intricacies, arose as a reference point of military greatness, generally because of the Nurmagomedov family's devotion to creating champions. The Birds MMA Club turned into an image of yearning, drawing in youthful gifts anxious to go through the extraordinary course of becoming heroes.

The Nurmagomedov family's devotion to making champions additionally appeared in their obligation to rewarding the local area. Magnanimous drives, instructive projects, and the development of a mosque in Abdulmanap's honor became expansions of their training reasoning. The most common way of creating champions, in this specific situation, reached out to making positive good examples and supporters of society.

Abdulmanap's part in making champions arrived at a powerful peak during Khabib's title session at UFC 254. Khabib's triumph was not only an individual accomplishment; it was a recognition for his dad and mentor who had died before that year. The close to home reverberation existing apart from everything else caught the substance of the familial bonds and the significant effect of Abdulmanap's training reasoning in making champions.

As the Nurmagomedov family's process go on with the development of the future, especially Umar Nurmagomedov, the story of creating champions endures. Umar, Khabib's cousin, ventures into the spotlight conveying the tradition of familial bonds, discipline, and enduring responsibility. The most common way of creating champions turns into a continuum, a living demonstration of Abdulmanap's persevering through impact on the family's training reasoning.

The many-sided course of creating champions inside the Nurmagomedov family unfurls against the scenery of a special social setting. Dagestan, with its rich embroidery of customs and a set of experiences saturated with wrestling, gives the fruitful ground where the imaginativeness of creating champions flourishes. The familial bonds, discipline, and obligation to combative techniques become intertwined with the social personality of the locale, making a story that reverberates a long ways past the limits of the octagon.

The social joining inside the training reasoning of the Nurmagomedov family is obvious in the adoration for conventional Dagestani rehearses. The lezginka, a conventional dance performed before battles, is an impactful representation of the indistinguishable connection among culture and the specialty of creating champions. The dance, with its cadenced developments and emblematic signals, is more than a pre-battle custom; it is an indication of social pride and a festival of the familial bonds that characterize the Nurmagomedov heritage.

Abdulmanap Nurmagomedov, as a social caretaker, comprehended the significant effect that social reconciliation could have on the most common way of making champions. The lezginka, performed for show as well as a profoundly imbued custom, turned into an emblematic extension between the old wrestling legacy of Dagestan and the cutting edge game of MMA. The familial bonds inside the Hawks MMA Club were fortified through these social works on, establishing a climate where warriors prepared together as well as shared a feeling of social personality.

The account of creating champions in the Nurmagomedov family is likewise profoundly weaved with the scenes of Dagestan. The tough landscape, where the family's process started, fills in as a figurative pot where discipline is produced and flexibility is tried. The actual difficulties of the climate become essential to the most common way of creating champions, imparting a durability that goes past the specialized parts of preparing. The contenders, formed by the requesting scenes of Dagestan, convey inside them the unyielding soul of the area.

Tales from the family's initial a long time in Dagestan portray the cooperative connection between the scene and the specialty of creating champions. Wrestling wasn't simply a game; it was a lifestyle formed by the shapes of the mountains and the soul of individuals. The familial bonds, shaped chasing greatness, were fortified by the difficulties presented by the regular habitat. Making champions in Dagestan, consequently, turned into a vivid encounter that drew from the actual texture of the locale.

The social combination inside the method involved with making champions reaches out to the otherworldly components of the Nurmagomedov family's excursion. The foundation of a mosque to pay tribute to Abdulmanap Nurmagomedov in Sildi, Dagestan, is a real, powerful sign of the entwining and the specialty of creating champions. The mosque, an image of profound dedication, turns into a space where the contenders track down comfort as well as draw motivation for their excursions.

Abdulmanap's instructing reasoning rises above the physical and the psychological; it digs into the profound domains that support the specialty of making champions. The mosque, in its development and importance, turns into a demonstration of the Nurmagomedov family's obligation to comprehensive turn of events. The contenders, in their quest for greatness, are not only competitors; they are people grounded in a profound grasping that supplements the physical and mental parts of their preparation.

The most common way of creating champions inside the Nurmagomedov family is likewise portrayed by a pledge to consistent learning and variation. The combination of different combative techniques disciplines into the instructing reasoning mirrors a receptiveness to development while keeping up with the guiding principle imparted by

Abdulmanap. The family's devotion to hand to hand fighting training turns into a powerful power that improves the most common way of making champions, guaranteeing that it stays important and successful in the steadily developing scene of MMA.

Stories from the Birds MMA Club feature the assorted impacts that add to the specialty of creating champions. The trading of information, inside the family as well as with contenders from different foundations, turns into a wellspring of aggregate development. The familial securities reach out past direct relations to envelop a worldwide local area of military craftsmen who share a typical ethos. The social reconciliation inside the club turns into a microcosm of the more extensive social trade that characterizes the Nurmagomedov family's way to deal with making champions.

The social coordination inside the most common way of making champions isn't restricted to Dagestan; it reaches out to the worldwide stage through the progress of Khabib Nurmagomedov in the UFC. Khabib's ascent to noticeable quality brought the practices and upsides of Dagestan into the worldwide spotlight, forming a story that goes past individual triumphs. The familial bonds and social pride turned into a general story that resounded with fans around the world, displaying the specialty of creating champions as an extraordinary and socially rich undertaking.

The story of making champions inside the Nurmagomedov family additionally digs into the job of difficulty in the formative cycle. Misfortune, whether as losses, wounds, or individual difficulties, turns into a pot that refines the personality of the contenders. Abdulmanap's instructing reasoning hugs difficulty not as an impediment but rather as an impetus for development.

The familial bonds inside the Falcons MMA Club offer a help framework that enables contenders to explore difficulties with strength and arise more grounded on the opposite side.

Stories from Khabib's vocation, especially the loss to Gleison Tibau and the difficulties paving the way to UFC 254, feature the family's way to deal with misfortune. The misfortunes and mishaps are not viewed as disappointments yet as any open doors for thoughtfulness and improvement. The specialty of making champions, in this unique circumstance, turns into an excursion of self-disclosure, where warriors advance as much from their losses as they do from their triumphs.

The Nurmagomedov family's devotion to social reconciliation inside the method involved with making champions reaches out to their generous undertakings. Magnanimous drives, instructive projects, and local area improvement projects are not only expansions of their outcome in the octagon; they are articulations of a more extensive obligation to social obligation. The specialty of creating champions, in this specific situation, turns into a comprehensive undertaking that points not exclusively to shape individual competitors however to contribute emphatically to the prosperity of networks.

One moving tale rotates around Khabib's visit to a neighborhood school in Dagestan, where the effect of the family's devotion to combative techniques and social mix becomes substantial. Seeing kids, anxious to learn and motivated by Khabib's excursion, embodies the groundbreaking force of the specialty of making champions. The familial securities, social pride, and obligation to schooling meet in minutes like these, making a permanent imprint on the local area.

The Nurmagomedov family's story of creating champions takes on an all inclusive aspect with the development of Umar Nurmagomedov, the cutting edge leading. Umar's process reflects not just the familial bonds and devotion to hand to hand fighting yet in addition the versatility expected to explore the intricacies of the advanced MMA scene. The specialty of creating champions, in this specific situation, turns into a continuum, a heritage that develops with every age while outstanding established in the immortal standards bestowed by Abdulmanap.

The specialty of creating champions inside the Nurmagomedov family is a layered and nuanced story that winds around together familial bonds, social coordination, flexibility, and a pledge to ceaseless learning. The scene of Dagestan, with its rich practices and testing landscapes, fills in as the setting for the family's excursion. The combination of social practices, profound aspects, and a commitment to social obligation hoists the specialty of making champions past the domain of sports. It turns into an extraordinary cycle that shapes competitors as well as people of character and supporters of the more extensive embroidery of human experience. The Nurmagomedov family's heritage in the specialty of creating champions isn't simply an account of triumphs; it is a demonstration of the getting through force of discipline, social pride, and the unfaltering quest for greatness.

2.1 In-depth examination of Abdulmanap's coaching techniques and training methods.

Abdulmanap Nurmagomedov, the patriarch of the eminent Nurmagomedov family, has made a permanent imprint on the universe of blended hand to hand fighting (MMA) through his imaginative instructing procedures and preparing techniques. His impact stretches out a long ways past the triumphs of his child, Khabib Nurmagomedov, in the UFC, venturing into the domains of discipline, mental guts, and the comprehensive improvement of competitors. A top to bottom assessment of Abdulmanap's training reasoning uncovers a nuanced approach that goes past the specialized parts of the game, incorporating social coordination, otherworldly aspects, and a guarantee to making champions as well as balanced people.

Fundamental to Abdulmanap's training procedures is the accentuation on discipline as a foundation of progress in MMA. The instructional meetings at the Birds MMA Club in Dagestan, under his authority, are eminent for their meticulousness and power. Discipline, in this unique circumstance, isn't simply a bunch of rules forced on the contenders yet a lifestyle that pervades each part of their preparation and self-improvement. Abdulmanap comprehends that making champions requires something other than actual ability; it requests a psychological discipline that can endure the difficulties of rivalry and life.

The discipline imparted by Abdulmanap isn't tyrant yet established in common regard and a mutual perspective of the objectives within reach. Warriors under his tutelage aren't simply following a mentor; they are important for a familial ethos where discipline turns into an aggregate responsibility. The instructional courses, set apart by their construction and concentration, are an impression of Abdulmanap's conviction that a restrained methodology is the establishment whereupon champions are fabricated.

One of the extraordinary parts of Abdulmanap's instructing procedures is the reconciliation of Dagestani social practices into the preparation routine. The customary Dagestani dance, the lezginka, performed before battles, is a powerful illustration of how social reconciliation turns into a unique component in the training reasoning. The dance is certainly not a simple custom; a custom interfaces the contenders to their social roots, imparting a feeling of satisfaction and solidarity. Abdulmanap perceives the mental effect of social combination, encouraging an outlook that rises above the actual parts of preparing.

The social reconciliation inside Abdulmanap's training reasoning reaches out past ceremonies to the fuse of customary Dagestani wrestling and hand to hand fighting strategies. The rich history of wrestling in Dagestan turns into a wellspring of information that illuminates the preparation strategies at the Falcons MMA Club. The combination of old procedures with present day approaches makes an exceptional mix that separates the Nurmagomedov family's instructing methods. The contenders get familiar with the most recent systems in MMA as well as draw from a centuries-old practice of battle sports that characterizes their social personality.

Abdulmanap's instructing procedures additionally dive into the otherworldly components of the competitor's excursion. The foundation of a mosque in Sildi, Dagestan, in his honor, is significant of the profound direction that supports his training reasoning. The mosque turns out to be in excess of a position of love; it is a safe-haven where contenders track down comfort, draw motivation, and develop an otherworldly versatility. Abdulmanap comprehends that the most common way of making champions includes supporting the body and psyche as well as the soul.

The profound aspects inside Abdulmanap's training methods are appeared in his capacity to bestow life illustrations through the game. Contenders at the Hawks MMA Club are not simply learning methods; they are retaining a way of thinking that rises above the octagon. Abdulmanap's lessons frequently integrate stories and accounts, drawing from his own encounters and the insight of Dagestani culture. The contenders, in their excursion, become competitors as well as people on a way of self-revelation and self-improvement.

A central part of Abdulmanap's training strategies is the versatility to the singular requirements and qualities of every contender. While there is an organized way to deal with preparing, he perceives the significance of fitting the training techniques to the extraordinary characteristics of every competitor. Whether a contender succeeds in striking, hooking, or a mix of both, Abdulmanap's training strategies are intended to upgrade their assets while tending to regions that require improvement. This customized approach mirrors his conviction that creating champions includes perceiving and supporting the singularity of every competitor.

The most common way of making champions under Abdulmanap's direction includes a complete way to deal with actual preparation. The instructional meetings incorporate a different scope of exercises, including striking, catching, molding, and competing. Abdulmanap puts an exceptional on flexibility, guaranteeing that his warriors are balanced competitors equipped for adjusting to different situations in the enclosure. The accentuation on a diverse range of abilities lines up with his vision of making champions who are experts in a single viewpoint as well as capable in all elements of MMA.

A fundamental part of Abdulmanap's instructing strategies is the joining of conventional Dagestani wrestling drills. Wrestling, profoundly implanted in the social texture of Dagestan, turns into a central structure block in the improvement of contenders at the Falcons MMA

Club. The drills center around method as well as on developing fortitude, perseverance, and mental sturdiness. Abdulmanap's way to deal with wrestling drills goes past the customary; it turns into a strategy for imparting strength and courage in his competitors.

The preparation techniques inside the Birds MMA Club likewise remember an accentuation for molding that goes past the ordinary cardiovascular exercises. Abdulmanap perceives the significance of mental perseverance in the unforgiving climate of MMA. The instructional courses are intended to push warriors as far as possible, genuinely as well as intellectually.

This comprehensive way to deal with molding mirrors his comprehension that making champions requires competitors who can stay cool headed and center under the most difficult conditions.

One more unmistakable component of Abdulmanap's instructing strategies is the usage of controlled competing meetings. Fighting, a basic part of MMA preparing, is drawn closer with an emphasis on method, system, and limiting pointless dangers. The controlled climate permits warriors to refine their abilities, explore different avenues regarding various methodologies, and foster a profound comprehension of battle elements. Abdulmanap's direction during fighting meetings isn't just about winning rounds however about picking up, advancing, and applying key reasoning to their specialty.

The familial bonds inside the Birds MMA Club assume a crucial part in Abdulmanap's training procedures. The brotherhood and common help among contenders add to a positive preparation climate. Abdulmanap cultivates a feeling of fraternity where every warrior's prosperity is commended all in all. The familial ethos goes past the actual preparation; it turns into a wellspring of everyday reassurance, inspiration, and shared development. This strong climate is a demonstration of Abdulmanap's conviction that creating champions includes supporting a local area of people who elevate one another.

Abdulmanap's training methods additionally reach out to the psychological part of the competitor's arrangement. Perception and mental symbolism are integrated into the preparation routine to improve concentration, certainty, and mental versatility. Contenders are urged to envision their triumphs as well as the difficulties they would experience in the enclosure. This psychological molding turns into a urgent part of Abdulmanap's training reasoning, setting up his competitors for the mental requests of high-stakes contest.

The training methods utilized by Abdulmanap Nurmagomedov likewise remember a sharp accentuation for technique and battle level of intelligence. Warriors are not simply prepared to execute methods; they are educated to think in a calculated way, examine rivals, and adjust their strategies progressively. Abdulmanap's training reasoning includes making figuring warriors who can pursue split-subsequent options in the disorder of the enclosure. The combination of system into the training strategies mirrors his conviction that making champions goes past actual ability; it includes creating insightful and strategically proficient competitors.

The training strategies inside the Nurmagomedov family likewise exhibit a guarantee to ceaseless learning and variation. Abdulmanap's responsiveness to consolidating bits of knowledge from different hand to hand fighting disciplines, combined with a receptiveness to developing methodologies, separates the Falcons MMA Club. The family's commitment to combative techniques training turns into a powerful power that enhances the training strategies, guaranteeing that they stay moderate and successful in the steadily developing scene of MMA.

One of the main attributes of Abdulmanap's training strategies is his capacity to impart versatility in his warriors. The warriors at the Falcons MMA Club are not protected from misfortune; they are ready to go up against it head-on. Abdulmanap's instructing reasoning hugs misfortunes as any open doors for development, and warriors are educated to gain from routs and arise more grounded. This flexibility turns into a characterizing element of his competitors, forming their professions as well as their way to deal with life's difficulties.

Abdulmanap's instructing strategies likewise include the fragile harmony between pushing contenders as far as possible and forestalling overtraining. The careful preparation of instructional courses, combined with a sharp comprehension of every contender's state of being, guarantees that the competitors are cresting brilliantly. Abdulmanap's way to deal with preparing force is estimated, perceiving that the drawn out wellbeing and manageability of his contenders' vocations are principal.

The training methods utilized by Abdulmanap reach out to the cornering procedures during battles. His presence in the corner isn't simply representative; it is a basic piece of the contender's psychological and consistent encouragement framework. Abdulmanap's quiet disposition and key direction become a balancing out force for his warriors, especially in high-pressure circumstances. His capacity to peruse the back and forth movement of a battle and give exact guidelines mirrors his abundance of involvement and profound comprehension of the game.

Abdulmanap Nurmagomedov's instructing strategies and preparing techniques likewise dig into the mental parts of battle sports, perceiving the meaning of mental grit chasing greatness. The psychological molding granted by Abdulmanap goes past getting ready warriors for the mental difficulties of contest; it is a far reaching way to deal with building a versatile outlook that stretches out into all features of life.

One critical part of the mental part of Abdulmanap's training procedures is the accentuation on perception and mental symbolism. Contenders are urged to clearly picture their triumphs as well as the difficulties they would experience in the enclosure. This psychological practice turns into an integral asset for building certainty, improving concentration, and getting ready for different situations. Abdulmanap comprehends that the brain is a strong partner in the excursion of creating champions, and his training strategies mirror a conscious work to bridle its true capacity.

The psychological molding inside Abdulmanap's instructing strategies stretches out to the improvement of a top dog's mentality.

Warriors are instructed to move toward difficulties with a mentality that embraces difficulty as a chance for development. Abdulmanap's training reasoning perceives that mishaps are an unavoidable piece of a warrior's excursion, and the capacity to defeat difficulty recognizes genuine bosses.

The psychological flexibility imparted by Abdulmanap turns into a main trait of his competitors, forming their exhibitions in the enclosure as well as their way to deal with life's difficulties.

One more mental aspect inside Abdulmanap's instructing methods is the development of an engaged and made outlook during contest. Contenders are prepared to stay under control during the most intense part of the conflict, settling on choices with clearness and accuracy. The capacity to remain mentally collected under tension is a sign of Abdulmanap's training reasoning, and his contenders frequently display an emotionless disposition even in the most extraordinary snapshots of a battle. This psychological discipline turns into a competitive edge, permitting contenders to explore complex circumstances with an elevated feeling of mindfulness.

The familial bonds inside the Falcons MMA Club contribute altogether to the mental versatility of Abdulmanap's contenders. The feeling of fraternity and common help makes a mental security net, where contenders realize they are in good company in their excursion. The kinship encourages a climate where competitors can share their contemplations, concerns, and weaknesses unafraid of judgment. Abdulmanap's instructing procedures perceive the significance of the mental emotionally supportive network inside the group, sustaining an aggregate outlook that builds up every contender's individual mental strength.

The mental arrangement inside Abdulmanap's training procedures is additionally clear in his way to deal with cornering during battles. His presence in the corner isn't just about specialized guidance; it is tied in with offering profound and mental help to his contenders. Abdulmanap's cool as a cucumber disposition reassuringly affects his competitors, assisting them with keeping up with their psychological concentration and certainty. His capacity to peruse the mental elements of a battle and proposition exact direction mirrors the profundity of how he might interpret the psychological parts of battle sports.

The instructing methods of Abdulmanap Nurmagomedov likewise reach out to the strategic and vital elements of MMA. His way to deal with procedure includes a careful examination of rivals, distinguishing shortcomings, and devising game strategies custom-made to every individual contender. Abdulmanap's training reasoning perceives that progress in MMA goes past actual ability; it requires a sharp comprehension of technique and the capacity to adjust to the developing elements of a battle.

One particular component of Abdulmanap's training methods is the combination of conventional Dagestani wrestling into the essential structure. The wrestling procedures, well established in the social legacy of Dagestan, give an exceptional munititions stockpile that separates his warriors. Abdulmanap's essential methodology includes utilizing the qualities of his warriors while taking advantage of the shortcomings of their adversaries. The capacity to consistently incorporate conventional procedures with current systems mirrors the versatility and development inside his instructing reasoning.

Abdulmanap's training procedures likewise address the strategic subtleties of various periods of a battle, including striking, catching, and changes. Contenders at the Hawks MMA Club are not prepared to be one-layered; they are furnished with a different range of abilities that permits them to direct the speed and style of a battle. Abdulmanap's training reasoning energizes flexibility, guaranteeing that his competitors are capable in all parts of MMA. This strategic variety turns into a competitive edge, permitting his warriors to adjust to different rivals and situations.

The training strategies inside the Hawks MMA Club likewise underscore the significance of battle level of intelligence (IQ) as a basic part of outcome in MMA. Abdulmanap imparts an essential outlook in his contenders, empowering them to think fundamentally, dissect rivals' developments, and pursue informed choices during battles. The capacity to peruse and respond to the steadily changing elements of a battle turns into a sign of his competitors, separating them as thinking warriors in the realm of MMA.

The flexibility inside Abdulmanap's training procedures is obvious in his openness to consolidating bits of knowledge from different combative techniques disciplines. The coordination of procedures from boxing, kickboxing, judo, and other combative techniques customs advances the range of abilities of his contenders, making them balanced competitors fit for dealing with assorted difficulties. Abdulmanap's obligation to consistent learning and transformation mirrors an instructing reasoning that develops with the game, guaranteeing that his contenders stay at the front of MMA advancement.

Abdulmanap Nurmagomedov's instructing strategies reach out past the limits of the preparation exercise center and battle field to include a guarantee to local area and social obligation. The family's commitment to magnanimous drives, instructive projects, and local area improvement projects is an indispensable piece of his training reasoning. Abdulmanap comprehends that the effect of his instructing goes past individual triumphs; it stretches out to elevating the local area and contributing emphatically to society.

One moving illustration of the local area centered part of Abdulmanap's training reasoning is the development of a mosque in his distinction in Sildi, Dagestan. The mosque turns into an image of profound and social pride for the local area, exemplifying the upsides of discipline, strength, and solidarity imparted by Abdulmanap's instructing strategies. The family's obligation to local area improvement mirrors a training reasoning that looks to make champions in the enclosure as well as supporters of the more extensive cultural texture.

Abdulmanap Nurmagomedov's instructing procedures and preparing strategies address a comprehensive and multi-faceted way to deal with the improvement of MMA competitors. His accentuation on discipline, social joining, otherworldly direction, and a guarantee to constant learning separates his training reasoning.

The mental flexibility, strategic sharpness, and versatility imparted in his warriors go past the domain of sports; they become fundamental abilities that add to self-improvement and achievement. Abdulmanap's training heritage, conveyed forward by the Nurmagomedov family, isn't simply a demonstration of the specialty of creating champions in MMA however a significant investigation of human potential, social character, and the getting through rules that characterize progress in any undertaking.

2.2 Highlighting the development of Khabib and other notable fighters under his guidance.

The improvement of warriors under the direction of Abdulmanap Nurmagomedov is a demonstration of his unrivaled instructing ability and the extraordinary idea of his preparation techniques. Boss among these warriors is Abdulmanap's own child, Khabib Nurmagomedov, whose excursion from a youthful Dagestani grappler to one of the best blended military specialists ever is a remarkable representation of the effect of Abdulmanap's instructing.

Khabib's formative direction under Abdulmanap's direction started in the natural scenes of Dagestan, where wrestling isn't simply a game yet a lifestyle. Since the beginning, Khabib was drenched in the social and military practices of his locale, establishing the groundwork for his future achievement. Abdulmanap's training procedures, well established in Dagestani wrestling, turned into the pot where Khabib's abilities and character were manufactured.

The familial connections among Khabib and Abdulmanap assumed a significant part in his turn of events. Past the mentor contender relationship, theirs was a dad child association grounded in shared enthusiasm and devotion to combative techniques. The lounge wrestling matches, where father and child took part in improvised meetings, weren't just about actual preparation; they were snapshots of holding and the transmission of generational information. Khabib's improvement as a contender was unpredictably woven with the familial ethos imparted by Abdulmanap.

Abdulmanap's instructing reasoning stressed discipline as the foundation of achievement, and this discipline became imbued in Khabib's way to deal with preparing. The thorough meetings at the Birds MMA Club, where Abdulmanap filled in as the lead trainer, were described by a requesting routine that improved Khabib's actual abilities as well as developed mental mettle. The discipline imparted by Abdulmanap was clear in Khabib's faithful hard working attitude and obligation to persistent improvement.

The combination of social practices inside Abdulmanap's training likewise assumed a huge part in Khabib's turn of events. The conventional Dagestani dance, the lezginka, performed before battles, was a custom as well as an impression of social pride and an association with the roots that characterized Khabib's personality.

The consistent coordination of social components into the preparation routine turned into a wellspring of solidarity for Khabib, supporting the familial and social bonds that supported his excursion.

Khabib's improvement as a warrior further features Abdulmanap's capacity to fit instructing procedures to the singular credits of every competitor. Khabib's wrestling foundation was flawlessly coordinated with striking and hooking strategies, making him a balanced competitor fit for succeeding in all parts of MMA. Abdulmanap's training reasoning, established in flexibility, guaranteed that Khabib's range of abilities was different and dynamic, permitting him to force his will on rivals with unmatched effectiveness.

The psychological molding conferred by Abdulmanap turned into a characterizing component of Khabib's battling style. The capacity to remain even-tempered under tension, settle on determined choices, and execute a strategy with accuracy were all signs of Khabib's methodology, mirroring the mental strength ingrained by his dad and mentor. The familial emotionally supportive network inside the Birds MMA Club, sustained by Abdulmanap, assumed a significant part in Khabib's psychological backbone, empowering him to explore the psychological difficulties of the game.

One of the significant minutes in Khabib's improvement came in 2012 when he confronted Gleison Tibau in a firmly challenged session. The battle, which tried Khabib's strength, finished in support of himself yet uncovered regions for development. Abdulmanap's reaction to the battle was meaningful of his instructing reasoning. Rather than harping on the triumph, he considered it to be a chance for development and learning. The loss to Tibau turned into a defining moment, forming Khabib's mentality and way to deal with the game under Abdulmanap's direction.

The key and strategic elements of Khabib's improvement were carefully created by Abdulmanap. The joining of customary Dagestani wrestling, combined with a sharp comprehension of MMA technique, made Khabib an impressive power in the lightweight division. Abdulmanap's capacity to devise game courses of action customized to explicit rivals and circumstances turned into a competitive edge that moved Khabib to unmatched outcome in the UFC.

The effect of Abdulmanap's training on Khabib's advancement is maybe most distinctively found in his undefeated spat the UFC. Khabib's predominance in the lightweight division, coming full circle in his title triumph, was an aggregate victory for the Nurmagomedov family and the Hawks MMA Club. The familial securities, discipline, and key discernment imparted by Abdulmanap turned into the mainstays of Khabib's prosperity, raising him to the situation with a world-wide symbol in the game.

While Khabib remains as the most renowned result of Abdulmanap's training, other outstanding warriors have likewise thrived under his direction. Contenders like Islam Makhachev, an individual Dagestani and a long-lasting preparation accomplice of Khabib, represent the congruity of Abdulmanap's instructing inheritance. Makhachev's improvement as a gifted lightweight competitor mirrors the persevering through standards and methods imparted by Abdulmanap inside the Hawks MMA Club.

The sustaining of youthful gifts inside the Birds MMA Club reaches out past direct relations, epitomizing Abdulmanap's obligation to local area and the more extensive improvement of Dagestani contenders. The rise of warriors like Umar Nurmagomedov, Khabib's cousin, and others from the area highlights the familial bonds and mentorship that characterize Abdulmanap's training reasoning. The tradition of improvement inside the Falcons MMA Club is a living demonstration of the getting through effect of Abdulmanap's training procedures on the up and coming age of warriors.

The tradition of Abdulmanap's training reaches out past the octagon, affecting the more extensive Dagestani people group and the worldwide view of combative techniques. The development of a mosque in Sildi, Dagestan, to pay tribute to Abdulmanap mirrors the entwining of profound qualities with his training reasoning. The mosque serves as a position of love as well as an image of the social and profound aspects implanted in the Nurmagomedov family's excursion.

Abdulmanap's instructing inheritance is additionally enlightened by the social obligation drives attempted by the Nurmagomedov family. Beneficent undertakings, instructive projects, and local area improvement projects are not only expansions of their outcome in the enclosure; they are articulations of a more extensive obligation to elevate the local area. The improvement of warriors inside the Hawks MMA Club is complicatedly associated with a bigger story of contributing emphatically to the prosperity of society.

In considering the improvement of contenders under Abdulmanap's direction, perceiving the family's commitment to social reconciliation and the conservation of Dagestani traditions is fundamental. The lezginka dance, the conventional wrestling strategies, and the joining of social practices inside the preparation routine exhibit a comprehensive way to deal with warrior improvement. Abdulmanap's instructing strategies are not bound to the specialized parts of the game; they include a more extensive vision that coordinates social character, otherworldly aspects, and a promise to social obligation.

The familial securities inside the Birds MMA Club keep on forming the improvement of contenders, encouraging a feeling of local area, common help, and shared development. The up and coming age of contenders, conveying forward the inheritance laid out by Abdulmanap, is a demonstration of the getting through effect of his instructing strategies.

The improvement of contenders isn't just a quest for individual progress in the enclosure; an aggregate excursion reverberates with the social pride, discipline, and familial ethos bestowed by Abdulmanap.

The proceeded with improvement of contenders inside the Hawks MMA Club, under the persevering through impact of Abdulmanap Nurmagomedov's instructing inheritance, stretches out into the domain of mentorship and the death of the light to the future. As the account of Khabib Nurmagomedov's cutthroat vocation arrived at its zenith with his retirement, the obligation of conveying forward the family's training customs tumbled to the arising abilities inside the club.

Umar Nurmagomedov, Khabib's cousin and a promising bantam-weight competitor, remains as an image of the continuous improvement under Abdulmanap's instructing ethos. Umar's process mirrors the consistent progress from the tutelage of Abdulmanap to the following period of the family's training inheritance. The mentorship given by Khabib, who has expected a training job himself, further highlights the progression of the familial bonds and the obligation to the standards ingrained by Abdulmanap.

The mentorship dynamic inside the Birds MMA Club exemplifies something other than specialized direction; it epitomizes the transmission of a social and philosophical legacy. Umar's improvement as a warrior includes refining his abilities inside the octagon as well as soaking up the upsides of discipline, flexibility, and social pride that have been necessary to the Nurmagomedov family's instructing reasoning.

The mentorship reaches out past direct relations to envelop a more extensive local area of contenders who have profited from Abdulmanap's instructing strategies. As Khabib changes into a training job, his initiative turns into an extension between the celebrated heritage laid out by his dad and the developing scene of blended hand to hand fighting. The Birds MMA Club turns into a center point of shared encounters, common help, and aggregate development, representing the familial ethos that has characterized Abdulmanap's instructing heritage.

The proceeded with improvement of warriors under Khabib's direction denotes another section in the Nurmagomedov family's training heritage. Khabib, having retained the insight and standards granted by Abdulmanap, presently fills in as a guide and mentor, encapsulating the qualities that have been the bedrock of their prosperity. The change from being a contender to expecting a training job is a characteristic movement, a demonstration of the family's obligation to sustaining individual heroes as well as a local area of competitors devoted to the quest for greatness.

The training strategies utilized by Khabib mirror a combination of his own encounters, Abdulmanap's lessons, and a receptiveness to development.

While maintaining the center standards of discipline, mental determination, and flexibility, Khabib presents a contemporary point of view that recognizes the consistently developing nature of the game. The mix of current preparation methods, vital experiences acquired from his own vocation, and a pledge to flexibility grandstand the dynamism inside the Birds MMA Club's training reasoning.

The continuous improvement of warriors inside the Hawks MMA Club likewise reaches out to the worldwide stage. The outcome of contenders like Islam Makhachev, a result of similar training genealogy, grandstands the widespread pertinence of Abdulmanap's standards. Makhachev's ascent in the lightweight division is a demonstration of the getting through effect of the family's training heritage past the limits of Dagestan. The Birds MMA Club turns into a signal for contenders looking for specialized skill as well as an all encompassing way to deal with their turn of events.

The worldwide reach of the Birds MMA Club is additionally intensified by the assorted foundations of the warriors who float towards its preparation grounds. The social coordination inside the club turns into a microcosm of the more extensive trade of thoughts and encounters that characterize the contemporary scene of blended hand to hand fighting. The Birds MMA Club isn't just a preparation office; it is a mixture of hand to hand fighting practices, cultivating a rich embroidery of learning, variation, and shared development.

The family's obligation to local area improvement and social obligation keeps on being a foundation of their training inheritance. Magnanimous drives, instructive projects, and commitments to nearby networks reverberation Abdulmanap's vision of hand to hand fighting as a vehicle for positive change. The improvement of contenders inside the Hawks MMA Club isn't confined from the more extensive cultural setting; it is unpredictably connected to a feeling of obligation towards elevating the prosperity of networks.

The development of a mosque to pay tribute to Abdulmanap in Sildi, Dagestan, remains as an actual sign of the family's obligation to profound and social qualities. The mosque turns into an image of progression, where contenders train their bodies as well as support their spirits. The combination of profound aspects inside the instructing heritage highlights the all encompassing methodology that goes past the details of the game.

The continuous improvement of contenders inside the Hawks MMA Club epitomizes a complex story that rises above individual triumphs and titles. It is an account of mentorship, progression, and a pledge to rules that characterize achievement both inside and outside the enclosure. Abdulmanap Nurmagomedov's instructing inheritance, conveyed forward by Khabib and the arising age, is a living demonstration of the persevering through force of familial bonds, discipline, and social pride.

The Falcons MMA Club stands as a preparation ground for contenders as well as a pot where the standards conferred by Abdulmanap keep on molding the predetermination of competitors, encouraging a local area devoted to the specialty of creating champions.

2.3 Interviews and insights from fighters who trained with Abdulmanap.

The meetings and experiences from warriors who had the honor of preparing under Abdulmanap Nurmagomedov give a significant look into the profundity of his instructing reasoning and the enduring effect he had on the people sufficiently lucky to be under his direction. These firsthand records address the groundbreaking idea of Abdulmanap's instructing strategies, the familial securities fashioned inside the Hawks MMA Club, and the persevering through inheritance that keeps on molding the vocations and lives of those he guided.

One normal subject reverberated by warriors who prepared under Abdulmanap is the accentuation on discipline as a central component of his training reasoning. Magomed Ismailov, a Dagestani contender who prepared at the Falcons MMA Club, takes note of that Abdulmanap imparted a degree of discipline that stretched out past the bounds of the exercise center. The organized instructional meetings, thorough actual schedules, and steady obligation to progress became vital parts of the warriors' day to day routines.

In interviews, warriors frequently talk about the all encompassing methodology taken by Abdulmanap in making champions. The instructional meetings weren't just about refining specialized abilities; they were vivid encounters that incorporated mental molding, social coordination, and profound direction. Umar Nurmagomedov, Khabib's cousin, underscores the way that Abdulmanap's instructing went past the actual parts of the game, forming warriors into balanced people fit for exploring the intricacies of life.

The familial bonds inside the Birds MMA Club are every now and again featured in interviews, outlining the feeling of fellowship and shared help cultivated by Abdulmanap. Warriors portray the rec center as in excess of a preparation office; it is a local area where shared objectives, triumphs, and difficulties are capable on the whole. This brotherhood adds to a positive preparation climate, making an emotionally supportive network that reaches out past the expert domain.

Abdulmanap's capacity to coordinate social practices into the preparation routine is a steady subject in interviews. Warriors frequently relate the meaning of customary Dagestani components, for example, the lezginka dance performed before battles. This social joining is certainly not a shallow part of preparing yet a well established practice that interfaces warriors to their legacy, imparting a deep satisfaction and personality.

The meetings likewise shed light on the versatility and customized approach that characterized Abdulmanap's training strategies. Contenders talk about how he fitted preparation projects to individual qualities and shortcomings, it is exceptional to perceive that every competitor. This customized approach guaranteed that warriors fostered a balanced range of abilities as well as sharpened their singular assets, adding to the different cluster of battling styles inside the Birds MMA Club.

The profound aspects implanted in Abdulmanap's training reasoning are clear in interviews with contenders who share their encounters. The foundation of a mosque in Sildi, Dagestan, in his honor is much of the time referred to as a demonstration of the otherworldly direction that pervaded the preparation climate. Warriors talk about the mosque as a position of love as well as a safe-haven where they tracked down comfort, motivation, and a more profound association with their motivation as competitors.

Khabib Nurmagomedov, in different meetings, gives experiences into the significant effect his dad's training had on his own turn of events. Khabib frequently stresses the psychological versatility ingrained by Abdulmanap, crediting his capacity to remain created under the gun to the mental molding got during preparing. The mentorship part of their relationship is tangible, with Khabib recognizing Abdulmanap as a mentor as well as a mentor and wellspring of motivation.

Warriors who prepared under Abdulmanap much of the time describe stories and illustrations that rise above the details of the game. These accounts frequently include anecdotes, platitudes, and astuteness established in Dagestani culture. Abdulmanap's lessons, shared during instructional courses, become basic to the contenders' excursion of self-revelation and self-awareness. Such tales feature the profundity of his training reasoning, which envelops the actual parts of battling as well as the more extensive embroidered artwork of human experience.

The meetings likewise shed light on Abdulmanap's training heritage with regards to contest. Warriors relate explicit systems, strategies, and cornering procedures utilized by Abdulmanap during battles. His presence in the corner is depicted as a strategic aide as well as a settling force that gives contenders a feeling of certainty and consolation during the most intense part of the conflict. The essential keenness bestowed by Abdulmanap stretches out past the exercise center, turning into a foundation of progress in high-stakes rivalries.

The versatility of Abdulmanap's instructing strategies is underlined in interviews talking about different periods of instructional courses. Warriors talk about the careful preparation, customized consideration, and the harmony among force and recuperation that described their arrangement. Abdulmanap's way to deal with cresting brilliantly, staying away from overtraining, and guaranteeing warriors are in ideal state of being for contests mirrors a nuanced comprehension of the requests of expert blended combative techniques.

In interviews, warriors offer thanks for the valuable open doors given by Abdulmanap's training. The opportunity to prepare under his direction is many times portrayed as an extraordinary encounter that reaches out past the actual game. Warriors credit Abdulmanap for molding their personality, imparting values that go past the limits of the enclosure. The feeling of appreciation and regard for his training techniques is substantial in their appearance on their time at the Birds MMA Club.

The worldwide effect of Abdulmanap's training is clear in interviews with warriors from assorted foundations who looked for preparing at the Falcons MMA Club. The draw goes past specialized skill; warriors talk about the novel mix of social coordination, otherworldly direction, and a feeling of local area that recognizes the exercise center. Abdulmanap's training inheritance turns into a signal that draws in competitors from around the world, making a mixture of combative techniques customs inside the Falcons MMA Club.

The meetings likewise give bits of knowledge into the job of mentorship in the continuous improvement of contenders inside the Birds MMA Club. As Khabib Nurmagomedov changes into a training job, warriors talk about the congruity of standards and values passed down from Abdulmanap to Khabib and presently to the future. The mentorship dynamic highlights the familial ethos that characterizes the instructing inheritance, making a heredity of direction and backing inside the club.

Proceeding with the investigation of meetings and experiences from contenders who prepared with Abdulmanap Nurmagomedov discloses a nuanced comprehension of the mentor's effect on specialized capability and mental flexibility. Warriors reliably accentuate the comprehensive idea of Abdulmanap's training, highlighting that his impact rises above the domain of game, penetrating different features of their lives.

A repetitive subject in the meetings is the fastidious consideration given to specialized perspectives during instructional meetings. Warriors review the accentuation on dominating basics, refining methods, and adjusting methodologies to individual styles. This obligation to specialized greatness turns into a sign of Abdulmanap's training, guaranteeing that warriors have a balanced range of abilities that can be sent really in the powerful climate of blended hand to hand fighting.

The coordination of customary Dagestani wrestling into the preparation routine is featured by contenders who quality their prosperity to the exceptional mix of strategies conferred by Abdulmanap. This joining isn't just about safeguarding social legacy yet about utilizing a rich repository of strategies that give an upper hand. Warriors offer thanks for the chance to learn and dominate these customary strategies, which become characterizing components of their battling styles.

The meetings likewise dive into the mental parts of preparing under Abdulmanap, uncovering how he imparted mental guts in his contenders. Accentuation on discipline, flexibility, and the capacity to face misfortune arises as key parts of his training reasoning. Warriors relate occasions where Abdulmanap's direction reached out past specialized guidance to give bits of knowledge into the psychological and personal difficulties of contest.

Warriors talk about the extraordinary force of Abdulmanap's inspirational methodologies. His capacity to move certainty, support self-conviction, and encourage a mentality of persistent improvement turns into a main thrust for warriors confronting the afflictions of expert contest. The tales partook in interviews feature minutes where Abdulmanap's words filled in as impetuses for beating difficulties, building up the possibility that his training stretched out past the actual domain.

The familial environment inside the Falcons MMA Club is a repetitive subject in the meetings, with warriors stressing the feeling of having a place and backing cultivated by Abdulmanap. This familial dynamic turns into a wellspring of inspiration and strength, with warriors sharing accounts of how the fellowship inside the group added to their prosperity. The Falcons MMA Club isn't simply a preparation office; it is an affectionate local area where warriors share a typical reason and aggregate desires.

Meets likewise shed light on the versatility and advancement inside Abdulmanap's instructing techniques. Contenders talk about his receptiveness to consolidating experiences from different combative techniques disciplines, taking into consideration a dynamic and moderate preparation climate. The incorporation of different strategies from boxing, kickboxing, judo, and different disciplines advances the warriors' ranges of abilities, mirroring Abdulmanap's obligation to remaining at the front of blended combative techniques development.

The otherworldly and social aspects inside Abdulmanap's instructing are featured as necessary parts of the preparation experience. Warriors examine the meaning of practices like the lezginka dance, as pre-battle customs as well as articulations of social pride and personality. The profound direction given by Abdulmanap, obvious in the development of a mosque in his honor, turns into an image of the further association between his training reasoning and the qualities imbued in Dagestani customs.

In interviews, warriors express a significant feeling of appreciation for the effect of Abdulmanap's training on their lives. Past the awards and triumphs in the enclosure, they confirm the self-awareness, versatility, and character advancement encouraged under his direction. The meetings become recognitions for a mentor whose impact stretched out a long ways past the specialized complexities of blended hand to hand fighting.

The development of the Hawks MMA Club as a worldwide center point for warriors looking for Abdulmanap's direction is a demonstration of the persevering through tradition of his instructing. Contenders from various corners of the world, with different foundations and encounters, meet at the exercise center to be important for an interesting instructing heredity. The meetings with these contenders represent the general allure of Abdulmanap's training reasoning, rising above social and topographical limits.

The mentorship part of Abdulmanap's training heritage is emphasizd in interviews with warriors who have changed into training jobs themselves. These people talk about the obligation they feel to convey forward the standards imparted by Abdulmanap and to add to the continuous advancement of the up and coming age of warriors. The mentorship dynamic makes a repetitive continuum of direction, guaranteeing that the substance of Abdulmanap's training reasoning perseveres.

The meetings and experiences from warriors who prepared with Abdulmanap Nurmagomedov give an extensive story of the significant effect he had on their vocations and lives. From specialized greatness to mental versatility, familial bonds, social incorporation, and profound direction, the tributes illustrate a mentor whose impact rose above the limits of traditional preparation. The getting through tradition of Abdulmanap's training isn't simply in the triumphs his warriors accomplished yet in the permanent imprint he left on the hand to hand fighting local area, molding the ethos of the Hawks MMA Club and impacting the direction of blended combative techniques on a worldwide scale.

Chapter 3

Beyond the Octagon

Past the octagon, the effect of Abdulmanap Nurmagomedov's instructing reasoning reaches out into domains that rise above the bounds of blended hand to hand fighting (MMA). His inheritance, woven into the texture of the Birds MMA Club, reverberates past the actual requests of battle sports, affecting society, local area, and the more extensive scene of Dagestan.

At its center, Abdulmanap's instructing reasoning rises above the prompt journey for titles and honors. It stretches out into the development of character, discipline, and a feeling of direction that arrives at a long ways past the spotlight of the octagon. The Hawks MMA Club turns into a pot where warriors are not just prepared to be champions in the enclosure however are molded into people who convey the qualities granted by Abdulmanap into each feature of their lives.

One of the conspicuous aspects past the octagon is the social incorporation inserted inside Abdulmanap's training reasoning. Dagestan, with its rich embroidery of customs and military legacy, fills in as in excess of a background; it turns into a vital piece of the contender's character.

The customary Dagestani dance, the lezginka, performed before battles, is certainly not a simple custom however a festival of social pride that resonates past the field. Abdulmanap's instructing rises above the actual parts of the game, turning into a vehicle for saving and advancing the social legacy of Dagestan.

The Falcons MMA Club remains as a demonstration of the force of hand to hand fighting as a binding together power inside a local area. Past the thorough instructional meetings, the exercise center turns into a get-together spot, a nexus where people from different foundations meet up with a common enthusiasm for hand to hand fighting. The fellowship cultivated inside the club stretches out past expert connections; it fashions enduring bonds that add to a feeling of having a place and common perspective.

Abdulmanap's instructing heritage likewise envelops a promise to social obligation and local area improvement. The development of a mosque in Sildi, Dagestan, in his honor embodies a significant association between otherworldliness, local area, and the combative techniques venture. The mosque isn't simply an actual construction; it turns into an image of the qualities imparted by Abdulmanap - discipline, lowliness, and a feeling of obligation to contribute emphatically to the local area.

The magnanimous drives embraced by the Nurmagomedov family and the Falcons MMA Club mirror a training reasoning that reaches out past individual accomplishment to a more extensive obligation to elevating those out of luck. Instructive projects, support for neighborhood drives, and commitments to local area government assistance projects underline a feeling of social obligation that lines up with the standards Abdulmanap tried to impart in his contenders.

One of the huge perspectives past the octagon is the mentorship job Abdulmanap expected as a mentor as well as a mentor. The familial bonds inside the Hawks MMA Club establish a climate where warriors track down specialized direction as well as basic encouragement and mentorship. Abdulmanap's impact as a coach is obvious in the stories of warriors who talk about the significant effect his insight, direction, and fatherly consideration had on their own and proficient turn of events.

The mentorship dynamic stretches out to the more extensive effect on Dagestani society. Abdulmanap's job as a coach to an age of warriors rises above the singular achievements of his understudies. The gradually expanding influence of his mentorship is felt in the development of contenders who, thusly, become tutors to the future, sustaining a pattern of direction and backing that heads past the limits of the exercise center.

Past the octagon, Abdulmanap Nurmagomedov's training reasoning digs into the profound components of combative techniques. The development of the mosque, referenced prior, is a sign of the family's obligation to profound qualities.

It turns into a space for supplication as well as for reflection, solidarity, and an indication of the greater rules that guide the combative techniques venture. The profound establishing inside Abdulmanap's training reasoning is a directing power that rises above the transient idea of triumphs and losses in the enclosure.

The Hawks MMA Club turns into a microcosm of the more extensive social trade inside the universe of blended combative techniques. The rec center draws in contenders from different corners of the globe, making a blend of hand to hand fighting customs, encounters, and points of view. The worldwide allure of Abdulmanap's training reasoning is apparent in the different foundations of the competitors who look for preparing at the Hawks MMA Club, encouraging a climate of culturally diverse comprehension and joint effort.

In the more extensive setting of Dagestan, Abdulmanap's training heritage becomes entwined with the area's social personality and worldwide discernment. The progress of contenders from Dagestan, sustained under Abdulmanap's direction, adds to a positive story that goes past games. Dagestan, frequently depicted from the perspective of its contenders' accomplishments, turns into a wellspring of motivation and pride for the nearby populace, exhibiting the groundbreaking capability of hand to hand fighting on a cultural level.

The effect of Abdulmanap's training reasoning is additionally clear in the self-awareness of contenders past their athletic professions. Contenders who progress into instructing jobs or add to the local area represent the getting through standards ingrained by Abdulmanap. The instructing genealogy inside the Falcons MMA Club turns into a conductor for passing down specialized mastery as well as a more extensive ethos of initiative, mentorship, and local area administration.

Abdulmanap's training heritage resounds in the stories of contenders who, post-retirement, convey forward the standards they guzzled under his tutelage. The change from being competitors to becoming envoys of hand to hand fighting and positive good examples highlights the enduring effect of Abdulmanap's instructing reasoning. The qualities imbued by Abdulmanap become core values that shape the direction of his warriors past their cutthroat years.

The instructive drives embraced by the Nurmagomedov family and the Falcons MMA Club expand the effect of Abdulmanap's training into the domain of information and ability advancement. The accentuation on schooling as a supplement to athletic preparation mirrors a comprehensive methodology that tries to engage contenders inside the enclosure as well as in their interests past the universe of blended hand to hand fighting.

The worldwide impression of Dagestan as a center point for hand to hand fighting greatness is an outer sign of Abdulmanap's instructing heritage. The progress of contenders from the district adds to a positive picture that difficulties generalizations and features the social extravagance and versatility of Dagestan.

Abdulmanap's training reasoning, well established in the district's customs, turns into an impetus for changing stories and encouraging worldwide appreciation for the different legacy of Dagestan.

The persevering through effect of Abdulmanap Nurmagomedov's instructing reasoning expands further into the domain of sportsmanship, moral lead, and the molding of a positive social story. Past the octagon, the Falcons MMA Club turns into a signal for a set of principles that focuses on regard, modesty, and uprightness, hoisting the game of blended combative techniques to a foundation of moral greatness.

One of the focal precepts of Abdulmanap's instructing heritage is the accentuation on sportsmanship. Contenders who prepared under him frequently think about the significance put on deliberately maintaining pride, both inside and outside the enclosure. Abdulmanap imparted in his understudies a profound feeling of regard for rivals, authorities, and the actual game. The illustrations learned in the rec center stretch out past contest, becoming core values that shape the personality of his warriors.

The accentuation on moral lead inside the Hawks MMA Club adds to a positive view of blended hand to hand fighting as a game established in discipline and fair play. Contenders from the club are not just known for their ability in the enclosure yet in addition for their praiseworthy way of behaving, setting a norm for sportsmanship that resounds inside the more extensive MMA people group. Abdulmanap's training reasoning turns into a power for changing the story encompassing the game, underlining its qualities past the exhibition of contest.

Abdulmanap's effect on the moral components of his warriors' lead is additionally obvious in their post-battle connections. Meetings and media commitment grandstand a degree of modesty and regard that rises above the typical bluster related with battle sports. Contenders from the Birds MMA Club become ministers for the game, typifying the standards of nobility and regard imparted by their mentor.

The Hawks MMA Club turns into a preparation ground for actual abilities as well as for the improvement of moral person. Abdulmanap's training reasoning consolidates an all encompassing methodology that perceives the interconnectedness of specialized ability and moral way of behaving. Warriors are prepared not exclusively to succeed in the game however to become good examples who rouse the future, encouraging a culture of uprightness inside the hand to hand fighting local area.

The moral underpinnings of Abdulmanap's training reasoning stretch out to the cornering and instructing procedures utilized during battles. Warriors frequently talk about the quieting impact Abdulmanap had in their corners, furnishing key exhortation with a disposition that reflected self-restraint and regard. The corner turns into a space where moral direct isn't compromised for triumph however is maintained as a fundamental part of the contender's excursion.

The more extensive effect of Abdulmanap's training reasoning is found in the groundbreaking impact on the view of Dagestan and its warriors. The district, frequently generalized and misconstrued, becomes inseparable from a type of competitors who encapsulate standards of honor, regard, and moral lead. Abdulmanap's instructing inheritance turns into a vehicle for social tact, testing previously established inclinations and encouraging worldwide appreciation for the social wealth of Dagestan.

The lowliness ingrained by Abdulmanap is especially significant. Warriors prepared under his direction frequently talk about the significance of staying modest, paying little heed to progress in the enclosure. The acknowledgment that triumph ought to be tempered with modesty and rout met with effortlessness turns into a sign of the Birds MMA Club. The lowliness developed inside the exercise center turns into a contrast to the bluster frequently connected with battle sports, introducing a more nuanced and grounded picture of MMA competitors.

The moral standards implanted in Abdulmanap's training reach out to the connections manufactured inside the Falcons MMA Club. The feeling of fraternity, common help, and fellowship cultivated in the rec center turns into a demonstration of the mentor's capacity to establish a climate where self images are saved for a long term benefit. Warriors become piece of a family, not simply colleagues, epitomizing a culture of regard and backing that reverberates inside the more extensive combative techniques local area.

Past the octagon, Abdulmanap's training reasoning tracks down articulation in the direct of warriors in their networks. The feeling of social obligation and moral conduct learned in the rec center turns into a main impetus for contenders to reward their networks. Altruistic drives, local area outreach projects, and commitments to nearby improvement projects become augmentations of the moral standards imparted by Abdulmanap.

The effect of Abdulmanap's training reasoning on moral lead is maybe most distinctively found in the worldwide view of the Birds MMA Club. The rec center stands as an image of another time in blended combative techniques, where specialized ability is supplemented by a guarantee to values that rise above the cutthroat field. Warriors from the Birds MMA Club become diplomats for a variant of the game that focuses on uprightness, lowliness, and moral greatness.

The mentorship dynamic inside the Hawks MMA Club assumes a significant part in the moral improvement of contenders. As Khabib Nurmagomedov changes into an instructing job, the standards granted by Abdulmanap keep on forming the moral direct of the future. The mentorship turns into a channel for the transmission of specialized skill as well as a general set of principles that characterizes the personality of contenders inside the club.

The moral direct of warriors past the octagon is likewise a demonstration of the enduring effect of Abdulmanap's instructing on their own lives. Meetings and profiles frequently feature the respectability, lowliness, and obligation to local area administration showed by previous understudies of Abdulmanap. The moral standards learned in the exercise center become directing lights that impact choices and activities a long ways past the extent of their athletic vocations.

The worldwide acknowledgment of Abdulmanap's training heritage as a model of moral lead adds to a positive change in the view of blended combative techniques. The account encompassing the game develops from being exclusively centered around actual ability to including the upsides of discipline, regard, and sportsmanship. Abdulmanap's instructing reasoning turns into an impetus for changing the more extensive discussion about the moral elements of battle sports.

Past the octagon, Abdulmanap Nurmagomedov's instructing reasoning makes a permanent imprint on the moral lead of contenders inside the Falcons MMA Club and the view of blended hand to hand fighting on a worldwide scale. The standards of sportsmanship, lowliness, and social obligation become vital parts of his instructing inheritance. The rec center becomes a preparation office as well as a cauldron where contenders are molded into people who encapsulate the most noteworthy moral principles, adding to a positive social story that reaches out a long ways past the serious field. The persevering through effect of Abdulmanap's training reasoning isn't bound to triumphs in the enclosure yet resounds in the person and lead of the warriors who convey forward his heritage.

3.1 Abdulmanap's contributions to martial arts beyond the world of MMA.

Abdulmanap Nurmagomedov's commitments to combative techniques stretch out a long ways past the domain of blended hand to hand fighting (MMA), including a rich embroidery of social, instructive, and cultural effect. His inheritance, woven into the texture of Dagestani hand to hand fighting practices, rises above the octagon, making a permanent imprint on the worldwide scene of battle sports.

At the center of Abdulmanap's commitments is his job in safeguarding and advancing the conventional combative techniques legacy of Dagestan. Established in a set of experiences that traverses hundreds of years, Dagestani hand to hand fighting, with its accentuation on wrestling, sambo, and different types of conventional battle, confronted the test of blurring into lack of definition despite present day sports. Abdulmanap arose as a torchbearer, committing his life to saving these customs as well as developing them to suit the contemporary setting.

One of his prominent commitments is the incorporation of conventional Dagestani wrestling strategies into the preparation routine of MMA contenders. While MMA is a cutting edge sport that joins different disciplines, Abdulmanap perceived the benefit of integrating the dependable methods of Dagestani wrestling into the munititions stockpile of his contenders. This essential combination turned into a characterizing element of the Hawks MMA Club's methodology, starting a trend for the joining of conventional hand to hand fighting into the developing scene of battle sports.

Abdulmanap's impact on Dagestani wrestling reaches out to the worldwide stage, where warriors from the Hawks MMA Club feature the adequacy of these methods in high-profile MMA contests. The progress of Dagestani warriors, a significant number of whom have a wrestling establishment molded by Abdulmanap, turns into a demonstration of the getting through importance and strength of conventional hand to hand fighting in the contemporary period.

Past the specialized viewpoints, Abdulmanap's commitments to hand to hand fighting remember a concentration for the social elements of Dagestani battle customs. The lezginka, a conventional Dagestani dance, isn't simply a pre-battle custom; it is a festival of social personality and pride. Abdulmanap's emphasis on integrating these social components into the preparation and pre-battle schedules of his contenders goes past the down to earth; it turns into an intentional work to respect and feature the rich legacy from which they draw motivation.

Abdulmanap's commitment to protecting social customs is additionally exemplified by the development of a mosque in Sildi, Dagestan, in his honor. The mosque turns into an actual indication of the profound and social aspects implanted inside his instructing reasoning. It remains as an image of the crossing point between hand to hand fighting, otherworldliness, and local area, supporting that the act of battle sports can be profoundly interlaced with social character and strict qualities.

The Falcons MMA Club, under Abdulmanap's direction, turns into a scaffold among custom and innovation. The rec center fills in as a course for the transmission of social practices starting with one age then onto the next, guaranteeing that the qualities inborn in Dagestani combative techniques are not lost in the consistently changing scene of sports. Abdulmanap's obligation to social conservation inside the setting of combative techniques starts a trend for a more all encompassing way to deal with preparing that goes past the details of battling.

Training arises as one more mainstay of Abdulmanap's commitments to hand to hand fighting. Perceiving the groundbreaking force of information, he puts serious areas of strength for on schooling as an indispensable part of a contender's turn of events. This obligation to scholarly development is clear in the foundation of instructive projects inside the Falcons MMA Club, furnishing warriors with chances to seek after scholastic greatness close by their athletic undertakings.

The instructive drives mirror Abdulmanap's conviction that a balanced individual is better prepared to explore the difficulties of life, both inside and outside the enclosure. The joining of scholastic pursuits inside the preparation climate turns into an interesting component of the Falcons MMA Club, testing the idea that actual ability and scholarly pursuits are fundamentally unrelated. This approach turns into a spearheading model inside the universe of battle sports, showing that the quest for greatness stretches out past athletic accomplishments to include scholarly strengthening.

The effect of Abdulmanap's instructive commitments reaches out past the quick setting of the Falcons MMA Club. Warriors who have profited from these drives become ministers for an all encompassing way to deal with preparing, motivating another age of competitors to esteem schooling close by their athletic interests. Abdulmanap's heritage in such manner isn't just the foundation of projects however the making of a social shift inside the combative techniques local area, empowering contenders to see themselves as researchers as well as competitors.

In the domain of cultural effect, Abdulmanap Nurmagomedov's commitments to hand to hand fighting are entwined with his obligation to local area advancement and social obligation. The foundation of beneficent drives, support for neighborhood undertakings, and commitments to the prosperity of Dagestan mirror an instructing reasoning that stretches out past the singular quest for titles to a more extensive feeling of obligation to elevate the local area.

The Falcons MMA Club turns into a center point for positive local area commitment, filling in as a stage for contenders to reward the districts that supported them. Abdulmanap's vision of combative techniques as a vehicle for social change becomes clear in the substantial commitments made by the club to neighborhood schools, emergency clinics, and other local area projects. The warriors, under his direction, become agents of Dagestani hand to hand fighting greatness as well as ministers for the groundbreaking capability of battle sports in encouraging local area prosperity.

The magnanimous drives embraced by Abdulmanap and the Hawks MMA Club are not symbolic motions; they address a way of thinking that sees combative techniques as a power for positive change. Whether it is supporting medical care framework, instructive projects, or drives pointed toward working on everyday environments, the club's association in local area advancement turns into an expansion of Abdulmanap's confidence in the limit of combative techniques to add to the improvement of society.

The effect of Abdulmanap's commitments to hand to hand fighting on local area improvement is maybe most piercingly communicated in the development of the mosque in Sildi, Dagestan. The mosque stands as a profound focus as well as an image of the interweaving of hand to hand fighting, social character, and social obligation. It turns into a reference point for the local area, epitomizing the upsides of discipline, modesty, and local area administration that characterize Abdulmanap's training reasoning.

The mentorship dynamic inside the Falcons MMA Club arises as a strong instrument for local area improvement. As warriors progress into instructing jobs, they become courses for the transmission of Abdulmanap's standards to the future. The mentorship reaches out past the specialized parts of battling to envelop the more extensive ethos of administration, obligation, and administration to the local area.

The worldwide acknowledgment of Dagestan as a center point for hand to hand fighting greatness, encouraged by Abdulmanap's commitments, focuses on sure the district. The outcome of Dagestani warriors on the global stage turns into a wellspring of motivation for the neighborhood populace, empowering a deep satisfaction and solidarity. Abdulmanap's heritage becomes entwined with the more extensive story of Dagestan, testing generalizations and adding to a more nuanced comprehension of the locale's social lavishness.

Abdulmanap Nurmagomedov's commitments to hand to hand fighting are additionally highlighted by his impact on the worldwide view of Dagestan as an impressive center for combative techniques greatness. Past the prompt effect on warriors inside the Hawks MMA Club, Abdulmanap's instructing reasoning adds to reshaping generalizations and cultivating a more nuanced comprehension of Dagestan's social lavishness and versatility.

The outcome of Dagestani warriors on the global stage turns into an important matter for the neighborhood populace. Abdulmanap's training heritage, as appeared in the accomplishments of warriors like Khabib Nurmagomedov, turns into a wellspring of motivation for hopeful competitors in the locale. The story shifts from survey Dagestan exclusively from the perspective of international difficulties to remembering it as a force to be reckoned with in the realm of battle sports.

Abdulmanap's commitments to hand to hand fighting assume a crucial part in testing and dispersing generalizations related with Dagestan. The worldwide impression of the locale, frequently formed by outer stories, goes through a change as Dagestani contenders grandstand their athletic ability as well as the upsides of discipline, regard, and modesty imparted by their mentor. Abdulmanap turns into a social representative, involving combative techniques as a medium to convey a story of solidarity, flexibility, and social pride.

The worldwide acknowledgment of Dagestan as a combative techniques force to be reckoned with lifts the district's status on the global stage. The progress of contenders from Dagestan turns into a place of festivity for the nearby local area and an image of positive portrayal. Abdulmanap's training reasoning, well established in the practices of the district, turns into a vehicle for social tact, rising above lines and cultivating a feeling of worldwide appreciation for the different legacy of Dagestan.

The effect on the worldwide impression of Dagestan isn't bound to the donning field. Abdulmanap's commitments stretch out to affecting how the area is seen socially and socially. The positive story made by the progress of Dagestani warriors challenges predispositions and advances a more extensive comprehension of the locale's commitments to the universe of combative techniques. The worldwide crowd starts to perceive Dagestan as a put on the guide as well as a social focal point with a rich history and a significant association with combative techniques customs.

Abdulmanap's instructing inheritance turns into an impetus for social trade inside the universe of blended hand to hand fighting. The Falcons MMA Club, under his direction, draws in contenders from different foundations, making a blend of hand to hand fighting practices, encounters, and points of view. The exercise center turns into a microcosm of the worldwide hand to hand fighting local area, cultivating a climate of multifaceted comprehension and coordinated effort.

The effect on the worldwide view of Dagestan likewise reaches out to the acknowledgment of Dagestani warriors as diplomats of their way of life. Contenders from the Birds MMA Club, outfitted with specialized ability as well as with a profound comprehension of the social qualities imparted by Abdulmanap, become delegates of a more extensive story. Their prosperity and direct all through the enclosure add to reshaping the story encompassing Dagestan, testing generalizations, and offering a more valid depiction of the district.

Abdulmanap's commitments to hand to hand fighting, consequently, reach out into the domain of social tact. The progress of Dagestani warriors turns into a type of delicate power, impacting how the world sees the locale and its kin. Abdulmanap's training reasoning, well established in the social texture of Dagestan, turns into a vehicle for cultivating worldwide associations and destroying assumptions about the district.

The mentorship dynamic inside the Birds MMA Club turns into a strong instrument for social trade. As warriors from various areas of the planet unite at the exercise center to prepare under Abdulmanap's direction, they become understudies of hand to hand fighting as well as social representatives. The trading of thoughts, customs, and encounters inside the rec center mirrors a dream of combative techniques as a general language that rises above social and geological limits.

Abdulmanap's impact on the worldwide impression of Dagestan is likewise apparent in the media inclusion and accounts encompassing Dagestani warriors. The accounts of devotion, discipline, and achievement become stories that resound past the universe of sports news coverage. The worldwide media, frequently instrumental in molding popular assessment, turns into a stage for displaying the positive parts of Dagestan's social legacy, as exemplified by the progress of Abdulmanap's training reasoning.

Abdulmanap Nurmagomedov's commitments to hand to hand fighting stretch out past the universe of MMA, winding around a story of social protection, instruction, and local area improvement. His job in coordinating conventional Dagestani hand to hand fighting into the contemporary setting of MMA starts a trend for the development of battle sports. The accentuation on schooling inside the preparation climate challenges regular standards, empowering warriors to seek after scholarly development close by their athletic interests.

Abdulmanap's obligation to local area improvement and social obligation changes the Hawks MMA Club into a stage for positive change. The magnanimous drives, support for nearby tasks, and commitments to the prosperity of Dagestan epitomize an instructing reasoning that sees hand to hand fighting as a power for cultural improvement. The mentorship dynamic inside the club turns into a vehicle for the transmission of specialized skill as well as a more extensive ethos of initiative, obligation, and administration to the local area.

The mosque in Sildi, Dagestan, remains as a demonstration of the otherworldly and social aspects implanted inside Abdulmanap's training reasoning. It represents the crossing point of hand to hand fighting, social personality, and strict qualities, supporting that battle sports can be profoundly entwined with more extensive parts of human experience. Basically, Abdulmanap's commitments to hand to hand fighting rise above the limits of the octagon, leaving a persevering through inheritance that improves the social embroidery of Dagestan and impacts the worldwide scene of battle sports.

3.2 His involvement in community development and promotion of healthy lifestyles.

Abdulmanap Nurmagomedov's effect rises above the limits of the hand to hand fighting world, venturing profoundly into local area advancement and the advancement of sound ways of life. His obligation to having a constructive outcome in the existences of individuals reaches out past the rec center, typifying a way of thinking that perceives the extraordinary force of sports and actual work in cultivating prosperity and local area union.

At the core of Abdulmanap's contribution in local area improvement is a significant feeling of social obligation. Perceiving the difficulties looked by his local area, he use his situation as a prestigious mentor to start projects that add to the general improvement of society. The Hawks MMA Club, under his direction, turns into a point of convergence for different local area improvement drives, exhibiting a dream that stretches out a long ways past the domain of serious games.

One of the outstanding undertakings that embodies Abdulmanap's obligation to local area improvement is the development of a mosque in Sildi, Dagestan, in his honor.

The mosque isn't simply a strict construction; it turns into an image of solidarity, otherworldliness, and a demonstration of the interconnectedness of hand to hand fighting, social personality, and local area administration. The mosque remains as a signal, both genuinely and emblematically, addressing the upsides of discipline, modesty, and a feeling of obligation to contribute decidedly to the local area.

Abdulmanap's effect on local area advancement is additionally apparent in the magnanimous drives attempted by the Nurmagomedov family and the Hawks MMA Club. The obligation to supporting nearby schools, clinics, and other local area projects mirrors a training reasoning that sees hand to hand fighting as a way to elevate the local area. These drives go past simple tokens of generosity; they exemplify a faith in the capability of sports to catalyze positive change at the grassroots level.

The Birds MMA Club turns into a center for positive local area commitment, offering a space for people to seek after their athletic yearnings as well as effectively add to the government assistance of the local area. Warriors from the club, under Abdulmanap's direction, become diplomats for local area advancement, taking part in and driving drives that address neighborhood needs. The rec center, as opposed to being exclusively a preparation office, develops into an impetus for social change, encapsulating Abdulmanap's vision of hand to hand fighting as a power for cultural improvement.

The mentorship dynamic inside the Hawks MMA Club assumes a critical part in local area improvement. As warriors progress into training jobs, they become channels for the transmission of Abdulmanap's standards to the future. The mentorship reaches out past the specialized parts of battling to envelop a more extensive ethos of initiative, obligation, and administration to the local area. Contenders turned-mentors become teachers in the game as well as good examples who motivate the cutting edge to embrace esteems that stretch out past the limits of the rec center.

Abdulmanap's contribution in local area improvement is portrayed by an all encompassing methodology that perceives the interconnectedness of actual wellbeing and in general prosperity. The advancement of sound ways of life turns into a focal fundamental of his instructing reasoning. Past the thorough instructional courses in the rec center, Abdulmanap underlines the significance of developing propensities that add to long haul wellbeing and imperativeness.

The Falcons MMA Club turns into a stage for advancing solid ways of life inside the local area. Abdulmanap's impact reaches out to wholesome schooling, stressing the meaning of a reasonable eating regimen and legitimate hydration. The warriors, as ministers for solid living, convey these standards into the local area, moving others to take on propensities that upgrade their general prosperity. The exercise center, in this way, turns into a nexus for the spread of information about the crossing point between active work, sustenance, and a solid way of life.

Abdulmanap's obligation to the advancement of solid ways of life is additionally reflected in drives that energize actual work past the domain of serious games. The Birds MMA Club, under his direction, arranges occasions, studios, and projects pointed toward drawing in the more extensive local area in exercises that add to actual wellness. This approach mirrors a comprehension that the advantages of sports and actual work reach out past the singular competitor to incorporate the prosperity of the whole local area.

The mentorship dynamic inside the Falcons MMA Club likewise assumes a critical part in imparting the significance of sound ways of life. Contenders, under Abdulmanap's direction, go through actual preparation as well as get training about the drawn out ramifications of their propensities on their wellbeing. This information turns into an establishment whereupon contenders, when they progress into training jobs, can impact the cutting edge to focus on wellbeing and prosperity as vital parts of their hand to hand fighting excursion.

Abdulmanap's association in local area improvement and the advancement of solid ways of life stretches out to instructive drives that enable people with information about actual wellbeing. The Hawks MMA Club, as a space that values scholarly development close by athletic pursuits, turns into a conductor for dispersing data about wellness, nourishment, and by and large prosperity. Instructive projects inside the exercise center add to a culture of wellbeing cognizance that penetrates the local area.

The effect of Abdulmanap's commitments to local area advancement and the advancement of solid ways of life isn't restricted to Dagestan; it resounds worldwide. The progress of the Birds MMA Club draws in contenders from various regions of the planet, making a different local area that shares a typical obligation to actual wellness and prosperity. The rec center turns into a microcosm of worldwide cooperation, exhibiting the general allure of Abdulmanap's training reasoning.

The worldwide acknowledgment of Abdulmanap's endeavors in local area improvement and the advancement of sound ways of life is additionally apparent in media inclusion and public talk encompassing the Falcons MMA Club. The accounts go past the accomplishments of individual warriors in the enclosure, featuring the positive effect the exercise center has on the local area and its obligation to encouraging solid living. This acknowledgment adds to a more extensive discussion about the social obligation of sports establishments and their capability to impact positive change.

Abdulmanap Nurmagomedov's contribution in local area improvement and the advancement of sound ways of life stretches out to the actual texture of the Hawks MMA Club, making a significant effect on the existences of people inside and past the rec center walls.

At the core of Abdulmanap's vision is a pledge to local area administration that goes past the common. The development of a mosque in Sildi, Dagestan, remains as an image of his devotion to otherworldly and local area prosperity. It isn't just a position of love yet a demonstration of the interconnectedness of combative techniques, social personality, and social obligation. The mosque turns into a social occasion point for the local area, encapsulating the upsides of discipline, modesty, and a common obligation to upliftment.

The magnanimous drives embraced by the Nurmagomedov family and the Birds MMA Club highlight a training reasoning that sees combative techniques as a power for positive cultural change. These drives, going from help for neighborhood schools to commitments to medical services framework, mirror a confidence in the groundbreaking capability of sports past the field. Abdulmanap's training heritage becomes entwined with local area improvement, epitomizing the possibility that progress in sports ought to convert into unmistakable advantages for the local area.

The mentorship dynamic inside the Hawks MMA Club assumes a significant part in the expansion of Abdulmanap's people group situated vision. As contenders progress into instructing jobs, they become torchbearers for the standards ingrained by their mentor. The mentorship stretches out past the specialized parts of battling to envelop a more extensive ethos of initiative, obligation, and administration to the local area. Contenders turned-mentors become teachers in the game as well as ministers for local area advancement, giving the light of social obligation to the future.

Abdulmanap's effect on local area advancement isn't restricted to infrastructural projects; it penetrates the actual culture of the Birds MMA Club. The rec center turns into a center point for positive local area commitment, offering a space for people to contribute effectively to the government assistance of the local area. Contenders, under Abdulmanap's direction, exemplify the upsides of discipline and modesty both all through the enclosure. The exercise center, as opposed to being exclusively a preparation office, develops into an impetus for social change, with warriors effectively partaking in and driving drives that address nearby necessities.

The worldwide acknowledgment of Dagestan as a center point for combative techniques greatness, cultivated by Abdulmanap's commitments, focuses on sure the locale. The outcome of Dagestani contenders on the global stage turns into a wellspring of motivation for the neighborhood populace, empowering a deep satisfaction and solidarity. Abdulmanap's inheritance becomes interwoven with the more extensive story of Dagestan, testing generalizations and adding to a more nuanced comprehension of the district's social extravagance.

Abdulmanap's contribution in local area improvement is portrayed by a comprehensive methodology that perceives the interconnectedness of actual wellbeing and in general prosperity.

The advancement of sound ways of life turns into a focal fundamental of his training reasoning. Past the thorough instructional meetings in the exercise center, Abdulmanap stresses the significance of developing propensities that add to long haul wellbeing and imperativeness.

The Hawks MMA Club turns into a stage for advancing sound ways of life inside the local area. Abdulmanap's impact reaches out to wholesome instruction, stressing the meaning of a decent eating regimen and legitimate hydration. The warriors, as diplomats for sound living, convey these standards into the local area, motivating others to embrace propensities that upgrade their general prosperity. The rec center, in this manner, turns into a nexus for the dispersal of information about the crossing point between actual work, sustenance, and a sound way of life.

Abdulmanap's obligation to the advancement of sound ways of life is additionally reflected in drives that empower actual work past the domain of serious games. The Falcons MMA Club, under his direction, arranges occasions, studios, and projects pointed toward connecting with the more extensive local area in exercises that add to actual wellness. This approach mirrors a comprehension that the advantages of sports and active work reach out past the singular competitor to include the prosperity of the whole local area.

The mentorship dynamic inside the Falcons MMA Club likewise assumes a crucial part in imparting the significance of solid ways of life. Warriors, under Abdulmanap's direction, go through actual preparation as well as get training about the drawn out ramifications of their propensities on their wellbeing. This information turns into an establishment whereupon contenders, when they change into instructing jobs, can impact the cutting edge to focus on wellbeing and prosperity as essential parts of their combative techniques venture.

Abdulmanap's contribution in local area improvement and the advancement of sound ways of life reaches out to instructive drives that engage people with information about actual wellbeing. The Falcons MMA Club, as a space that values scholarly development close by athletic pursuits, turns into a conductor for dispersing data about wellness, sustenance, and generally speaking prosperity. Instructive projects inside the rec center add to a culture of wellbeing cognizance that penetrates the local area.

The effect of Abdulmanap's commitments to local area advancement and the advancement of sound ways of life isn't restricted to Dagestan; it resounds around the world. The outcome of the Birds MMA Club draws in contenders from various regions of the planet, making a different local area that shares a typical obligation to actual wellness and prosperity. The rec center turns into a microcosm of worldwide coordinated effort, displaying the general allure of Abdulmanap's training reasoning.

The worldwide acknowledgment of Abdulmanap's endeavors in local area improvement and the advancement of solid ways of life is additionally obvious in media inclusion and public talk encompassing the Hawks MMA Club.

The accounts go past the accomplishments of individual warriors in the enclosure, featuring the positive effect the exercise center has on the local area and its obligation to encouraging sound living. This acknowledgment adds to a more extensive discussion about the social obligation of sports organizations and their capability to impact positive change.

Abdulmanap Nurmagomedov's contribution in local area improvement and the advancement of solid ways of life represents a training reasoning that reaches out past the domain of serious games. The development of a mosque, beneficent drives, and backing for neighborhood projects highlight a pledge to cultural prosperity. The Hawks MMA Club, under Abdulmanap's direction, turns into an impetus for positive local area commitment, exemplifying upsides of discipline, lowliness, and a feeling of obligation to inspire the local area.

Abdulmanap's effect on the advancement of solid ways of life goes past the actual preparation in the rec center. The accentuation on sustenance, instructive projects, and local area commitment mirrors a comprehensive way to deal with prosperity. The rec center turns into a stage for dispersing information about the convergence of active work, sustenance, and by and large wellbeing. Abdulmanap's heritage, thusly, isn't just in the triumphs accomplished in the enclosure yet in the positive and persevering through influence on the wellbeing and prosperity of people and networks, both locally and universally.

3.3 Exploration of his impact on the broader sports community.
Abdulmanap Nurmagomedov's effect on the more extensive games local area stretches out a long ways past the limits of blended hand to hand fighting (MMA), rising above disciplines and impacting the ethos of training, mentorship, and sportsmanship on a worldwide scale. His inheritance resounds as a guide of motivation, forming the story of being a mentor, a tutor, and a supporter of the universe of sports.

At the center of Abdulmanap's impact is his instructing reasoning, portrayed by a comprehensive methodology that goes past specialized preparing. The Hawks MMA Club, under his direction, turns into a research center for developing talented warriors as well as balanced people. This approach difficulties the generalization of battle sports as exclusively actual undertakings, accentuating the significance of character advancement, discipline, and scholarly development.

Abdulmanap's effect on the more extensive games local area is apparent in the outcome of his contenders, especially his child, Khabib Nurmagomedov, who arises as quite possibly of the most predominant player throughout the entire existence of MMA. The accomplishments of Dagestani warriors under Abdulmanap's tutelage grandstand an instructing procedure that mixes conventional hand to hand fighting with current strategies. The worldwide acknowledgment of these accomplishments adds to a reexamination of training works on, stressing the significance of a balanced, socially grounded approach.

The mentorship dynamic inside the Falcons MMA Club turns into a model for cultivating positive connections among mentors and competitors. Abdulmanap's job as a guide reaches out past the specialized parts of battling to incorporate the more extensive improvement of character, strength, and a feeling of obligation. This mentorship dynamic difficulties the cliché picture of mentors exclusively as tacticians, underlining their essential job in deeply shaping the existences of competitors both inside and outside the brandishing field.

Abdulmanap's effect on the more extensive games local area additionally reaches out to the advancement of social mindfulness and variety. The Birds MMA Club draws in contenders from various corners of the globe, establishing a multicultural climate inside the rec center. This variety turns into a demonstration of the widespread allure of Abdulmanap's training reasoning, displaying that greatness in hand to hand fighting rises above social and geological limits.

The outcome of Dagestani warriors on the global stage, impelled by Abdulmanap's training, challenges generalizations related with specific locales and identities. The worldwide acknowledgment of Dagestan as a center for hand to hand fighting greatness reshapes stories about the Caucasus locale, underscoring its social wealth, versatility, and commitments to the worldwide games local area. Abdulmanap's heritage becomes entwined with the more extensive discussion about variety and portrayal in sports.

Abdulmanap Nurmagomedov's effect on the more extensive games local area is additionally exemplified by his commitments to the advancement of training techniques. His combination of customary Dagestani wrestling methods into the preparation routine of MMA warriors starts a trend for the combination of conventional combative techniques with contemporary games. This approach becomes compelling in the more extensive scene of battle sports, empowering mentors to investigate the rich embroidery of conventional methods.

The accentuation on instruction inside the preparation climate of the Hawks MMA Club difficulties ordinary standards inside the games local area. Abdulmanap's obligation to scholarly development as a necessary piece of a warrior's improvement adds to a change in perspective, empowering competitors to seek after scholastic greatness close by their athletic undertakings. This approach difficulties generalizations about competitors' scholarly capacities and highlights the significance of developing a balanced character past games.

Abdulmanap's effect stretches out to forming the discussion about the moral components of battle sports. His training reasoning, established in standards of discipline, regard, and sportsmanship, turns into a benchmark for moral lead inside the more extensive games local area. The worldwide acknowledgment of Abdulmanap's training heritage adds to a positive change in the view of MMA, exhibiting that combative techniques can exemplify values that go past simple actual ability.

The Falcons MMA Club turns into a stage for cultivating local area commitment, testing the idea that sports organizations exist in confinement from more extensive cultural worries. Abdulmanap's obligation to local area improvement and social obligation fills in as a model for sports associations around the world. The beneficent drives, support for nearby undertakings, and commitments to the prosperity of Dagestan epitomize a training reasoning that perspectives sports as a vehicle for positive cultural change.

Abdulmanap's effect on the more extensive games local area is additionally obvious in the media inclusion and stories encompassing Dagestani contenders. The tales of devotion, discipline, and achievement become stories that reverberate past the universe of sports newscasting. The worldwide media, frequently instrumental in molding general assessment, turns into a stage for displaying the positive parts of Dagestan's social legacy, as exemplified by the outcome of Abdulmanap's training reasoning.

His impact on the more extensive games local area is highlighted by the getting through acknowledgment of his training reasoning even past his lifetime. Mentors and competitors from different disciplines keep on drawing motivation from Abdulmanap's accentuation on social establishing, mentorship, and moral lead. His heritage turns into a standard for those trying to rethink progress in sports concerning triumphs as well as with regards to the positive effect on people and networks.

Abdulmanap Nurmagomedov's effect on the more extensive games local area unfurls as a multi-layered story that envelops the specialized parts of training as well as the significant effect on social mindfulness, morals, and local area commitment. His heritage reverberates as a demonstration of the extraordinary force of sports past the quick field, making a permanent imprint on the way mentors, competitors, and sports establishments approach their jobs inside the more extensive cultural setting.

In the domain of training procedures, Abdulmanap's imaginative coordination of customary Dagestani wrestling methods into the preparation of MMA contenders turns into a worldview for the development of battle sports. This approach addresses a union of exceptionally old hand to hand fighting customs with the requests of current rivalry. Mentors across different disciplines observe, perceiving the benefit of investigating customary methods and adjusting them to contemporary games settings.

Abdulmanap's accentuation on schooling inside the preparation climate challenges the predominant standards inside the games local area. The Birds MMA Club turns into a reference point for competitors chasing after scholarly development close by their actual turn of events. This nuanced approach difficulties generalizations about the mental abilities of competitors and highlights the significance of developing balanced people. Mentors around the world, motivated by this way of thinking, begin rethinking the job of training in the all encompassing improvement of competitors.

The mentorship dynamic inside the Falcons MMA Club turns into a wellspring of motivation for mentors trying to rethink their jobs past strategic guidance. Abdulmanap's impact reaches out a long ways past the bounds of the exercise center, underlining the job of mentors as guides and powerhouses in the existences of their competitors. The mentorship model, described by standards of discipline, flexibility, and a feeling of obligation, prompts a more extensive discussion inside the games local area about the moral elements of instructing.

The effect of Abdulmanap on the games local area isn't restricted to MMA; it reaches out to battle sports by and large, cultivating a reconsideration of values and morals inside these disciplines. His training reasoning, established in standards of regard and sportsmanship, turns into a benchmark for moral direct inside the more extensive games scene. Mentors and competitors from different disciplines focus on Abdulmanap's inheritance as an aide for imparting values that go past the quest for triumph.

The Falcons MMA Club's job as a stage for local area commitment turns into a reference point for sports associations around the world. Abdulmanap's obligation to local area improvement and social obligation starts a trend for sports establishments to effectively add to the government assistance of the networks they serve. The magnanimous drives, support for nearby ventures, and commitments to the prosperity of Dagestan become a plan for sports associations looking to incorporate a feeling of social obligation into their missions.

Abdulmanap's effect on the more extensive games local area is reverberated in the media inclusion and accounts encompassing Dagestani warriors. The accounts of commitment, discipline, and achievement become more than sports stories — they become stories of motivation with more extensive cultural ramifications. The worldwide media, frequently compelling in molding popular assessment, turns into a channel for displaying the positive parts of Dagestan's social legacy, testing generalizations, and adding to a more nuanced comprehension of the locale.

His heritage perseveres as mentors and competitors from different disciplines keep on drawing motivation from his training reasoning. The worldwide games local area perceives that progress in sports would be able and ought to be estimated by triumphs in the ring as well as by the positive effect on people and networks. Abdulmanap Nurmagomedov turns into an image for a groundbreaking way to deal with sports — one that underscores the significance of social establishing, mentorship, moral direct, and local area commitment.

Abdulmanap Nurmagomedov's effect on the more extensive games local area is a story of development, social wealth, morals, and local area commitment. His training reasoning turns into a directing light for mentors and competitors, motivating a reconsideration of conventional standards inside the games scene.

The Falcons MMA Club, under his direction, turns into a model for local area situated sports associations, exhibiting the positive impact that sports can have past the field. Abdulmanap's heritage stretches out past the octagon, adding to a worldwide discussion about the groundbreaking force of sports in molding people and networks to improve things.

Chapter 4

Triumphs and Challenges

The excursion of Abdulmanap Nurmagomedov, set apart by wins and difficulties, fills in as an enamoring story that rises above the bounds of the octagon. As a loved mentor, coach, and patriarch, his biography is an investigation of diligence, social versatility, and the extraordinary force of combative techniques.

Wins describe Abdulmanap's story, and at the very front is the exceptional outcome of his warriors, especially his child, Khabib Nurmagomedov, in the realm of blended hand to hand fighting (MMA). Khabib's ascent to turn into an undefeated UFC lightweight hero is a demonstration of the viability of Abdulmanap's instructing reasoning. The triumphs in the enclosure are not simply individual victories; they address the climax of long stretches of devoted preparing, mentorship, and a profound association with the social foundations of Dagestan.

The outcome of Dagestani contenders under Abdulmanap's tutelage challenges assumptions about the locale, offering a story of solidarity, discipline, and strength that goes past international accounts. Dagestan, frequently connected with difficulties, turns into an image of combative techniques greatness and a wellspring of motivation for hopeful warriors internationally.

The victories of Abdulmanap's warriors add to reshaping world-wide discernments about Dagestan, displaying the positive parts of its social legacy.

Abdulmanap's training strategy, well established in the conventional hand to hand fighting of Dagestan, turns into a victory of saving social legacy even with present day challenges. The coordination of customary wrestling strategies into the preparation routine of MMA contenders prompts outcome in the octagon as well as highlights the ageless adequacy of these procedures. This win turns into a story of development inside custom, testing the division among old and contemporary combative techniques.

Past the field, Abdulmanap's victories manifest in the mentorship dynamic inside the Falcons MMA Club. His impact stretches out past the specialized parts of battling to incorporate the more extensive improvement of character, strength, and a feeling of obligation. Warriors under his direction become ministers for Dagestan as well as for the upsides of discipline, regard, and modesty imparted by their mentor. The mentorship win turns into a groundbreaking power that shapes effective competitors as well as balanced people.

In any case, the way to win is frequently cleared with difficulties, and Abdulmanap's process is no exemption. One of the persevering through difficulties is the international scene of Dagestan, set apart by verifiable intricacies and contemporary issues. The district's international difficulties become piece of the story, forming the flexibility and assurance of its kin, including Abdulmanap and his contenders. The victories accomplished inside the donning field become a wellspring of pride and strength despite more extensive difficulties.

Abdulmanap's obligation to safeguarding social legacy faces difficulties with regards to a quickly impacting world. The conventional hand to hand fighting of Dagestan, while successful, are in danger of being eclipsed by globalized patterns in battle sports. Adjusting custom and innovation turns into a sensitive test, requiring key transformation without compromising the basic beliefs that characterize Dagestani combative techniques. The victory over this challenge lies in Abdulmanap's capacity to coordinate custom with development, making an exceptional mix that reverberates on the worldwide stage.

The international difficulties of Dagestan are reflected in the accounts encompassing its contenders. The outcome of Dagestani contenders, while celebrated universally, isn't without its intricacies. Generalizations and misinterpretations about the district continue, and the victories accomplished inside the octagon become a type of social discretion, testing assumptions about Dagestan. Abdulmanap's training reasoning turns into a vehicle for reshaping stories and encouraging a more nuanced comprehension of the locale's social extravagance.

One of the strong difficulties Abdulmanap faces is the individual misfortune of losing his child and star student, Abdulmanap Nurmagomedov.

The unfavorable demise of Khabib sends shockwaves through the MMA people group and resounds profoundly inside the Nurmagomedov family. This significant misfortune turns into a stupendous test, testing the versatility and strength of Abdulmanap as a mentor, father, and patriarch. The victory over this profoundly private test is a demonstration of Abdulmanap's inward guts and his enduring obligation to the rules that characterize his instructing reasoning.

The mentorship dynamic inside the Birds MMA Club, while a wellspring of win, likewise presents difficulties. The obligation of shaping the existences of youthful competitors accompanies the heaviness of assumptions and the intricacies of self-improvement. Abdulmanap's job as a tutor isn't without its preliminaries, requiring a sensitive harmony among direction and permitting people to explore their own ways. The victory lies in the positive effect on the existences of his warriors, yet it is an excursion set apart by the difficulties of mentorship in a dynamic and developing games scene.

In the midst of these victories and difficulties, Abdulmanap Nurmagomedov's process fills in as a microcosm of the more extensive human experience. His story epitomizes the complexities of social safeguarding, the effect of international scenes, the sensitive harmony among custom and advancement, and the significant individual difficulties that shape a singular's personality. Abdulmanap's story turns into an all inclusive story of strength, assurance, and the groundbreaking force of sports and mentorship.

The international difficulties of Dagestan, set apart by verifiable intricacies and contemporary issues, shape the story of Abdulmanap's excursion. Dagestan's set of experiences, impacted by its area at the junction of Eastern Europe and Western Asia, turns into a scenery to the difficulties looked by its kin. Abdulmanap's victories inside the domain of sports become a type of social tact, testing generalizations and offering a positive story about the locale. The international difficulties become piece of the more extensive story, interweaving with the individual and expert excursion of Abdulmanap.

Despite international difficulties, Abdulmanap's instructing reasoning turns into a reference point of social strength. The coordination of customary Dagestani wrestling strategies into the universe of MMA grandstands the immortal viability of these techniques. The victory lies in triumphs inside the enclosure as well as in the protection of social legacy. Abdulmanap turns into an overseer of custom, exploring the difficulties of an influencing world while remaining consistent with the rules that characterize Dagestani hand to hand fighting.

The individual misfortune of losing his child, Abdulmanap Nurmagomedov, turns into a fantastic test that rises above the brandishing field. The unfavorable passing sends shockwaves through the MMA people group and resounds profoundly inside the Nurmagomedov family. This significant misfortune tests Abdulmanap's versatility, provoking him to track down importance and reason in the midst of sadness.

The victory over this profoundly private test turns into a demonstration of his internal strength and the persevering through tradition of his instructing reasoning.

The mentorship dynamic inside the Birds MMA Club, while a wellspring of win, likewise presents difficulties. The obligation of deeply shaping the existences of youthful competitors accompanies the heaviness of assumptions and the intricacies of self-improvement. Abdulmanap's job as a coach isn't without its preliminaries, requiring a fragile harmony among direction and permitting people to explore their own ways. The victory lies in the positive effect on the existences of his warriors, however it is an excursion set apart by the difficulties of mentorship in a dynamic and developing games scene.

In the midst of these victories and difficulties, Abdulmanap Nurmagomedov's process fills in as a microcosm of the more extensive human experience. His story typifies the complexities of social protection, the effect of international scenes, the sensitive harmony among custom and advancement, and the significant individual difficulties that shape a singular's personality. Abdulmanap's story turns into a general story of strength, assurance, and the extraordinary force of sports and mentorship.

Abdulmanap Nurmagomedov's excursion, set apart by wins and difficulties, unfurls as a rich story that digs into the intricacies of individual, social, and wearing aspects. Past the octagon, his story turns into a demonstration of the human soul, the getting through force of mentorship, and the unique interaction among custom and development.

The international difficulties of Dagestan, where Abdulmanap hails from, are unpredictably woven into the texture of his excursion. Dagestan's set of experiences, described by its situation at the junction of Eastern Europe and Western Asia, mirrors an embroidery of social variety and verifiable intricacies. This international setting shapes the strength and assurance of its kin, making an exceptional setting for Abdulmanap's victories and difficulties.

Dagestan, frequently depicted from international perspectives that feature its difficulties, goes through a change in the story molded by Abdulmanap's training reasoning. The progress of Dagestani contenders in the worldwide field turns into a wellspring of pride and strength, testing winning generalizations. Abdulmanap's training reasoning arises as a type of social strategy, offering a positive story about the district's social extravagance and the strength got from its hand to hand fighting customs.

The coordination of conventional Dagestani wrestling methods into the universe of MMA addresses a victory over the test of saving social legacy in the midst of a quickly impacting world. This combination of custom and innovation turns into a sign of Abdulmanap's training theory. The ageless adequacy of customary methods becomes obvious in the outcome of his contenders, displaying that advancement inside custom can prompt victories in sports as well as in social safeguarding.

Abdulmanap's process is set apart by a promise to offsetting custom with development, exploring the fragile dance between saving social legacy and adjusting to the requests of the contemporary games scene. The test lies in finding some kind of harmony without weakening the substance of Dagestani combative techniques. Abdulmanap's capacity to explore this challenge turns into a victory that reaches out past the octagon, adding to a nuanced comprehension of how custom can coincide with development in the domain of sports.

The individual misfortune of losing his child, Abdulmanap Nurmagomedov, is a test that rises above the brandishing field, venturing into the profundities of the human experience. The unfavorable demise of Khabib sends shockwaves through the MMA people group and resonates profoundly inside the Nurmagomedov family. This significant misfortune tests Abdulmanap's versatility, moving him to track down importance and reason in the midst of despondency. The victory over this profoundly private test turns into a demonstration of his inward strength and the persevering through tradition of his instructing reasoning.

Abdulmanap's mentorship dynamic inside the Falcons MMA Club, while a wellspring of win, isn't without its difficulties. The obligation of profoundly shaping the existences of youthful competitors accompanies the heaviness of assumptions and the intricacies of self-improvement. Abdulmanap's job as a tutor requires a sensitive harmony between giving direction and permitting people to explore their own ways. This mentorship challenge is an excursion set apart by the intricacies of significantly shaping the existences of youthful competitors in a dynamic and developing games scene.

The mentorship win lies in the positive effect on the existences of his contenders. Past the triumphs in the enclosure, the persevering through connections manufactured inside the Falcons MMA Club become a demonstration of the extraordinary force of mentorship. Abdulmanap's mentorship goes past the specialized parts of battling; it incorporates the more extensive improvement of character, versatility, and a feeling of obligation. The victory lies in the production of a local area that stretches out past the exercise center, where warriors become talented competitors as well as people molded by the qualities imparted by their mentor.

The getting through international difficulties of Dagestan, set apart by authentic intricacies and contemporary issues, are background as well as indispensable to Abdulmanap's story. The victories accomplished inside the octagon become a wellspring of pride and versatility notwithstanding more extensive difficulties. Abdulmanap's training reasoning, established in the customs of Dagestani combative techniques, turns into a type of social strategy that difficulties generalizations and offers a positive story about the locale.

The coordination of conventional Dagestani wrestling methods into the universe of MMA addresses a victory over the test of saving social legacy in the midst of a quickly impacting world. This combination of custom and innovation turns into a sign of Abdulmanap's training theory.

The ageless adequacy of customary methods becomes obvious in the outcome of his contenders, displaying that advancement inside custom can prompt victories in sports as well as in social safeguarding.

Abdulmanap's process is set apart by a promise to offsetting custom with development, exploring the fragile dance between saving social legacy and adjusting to the requests of the contemporary games scene. The test lies in finding some kind of harmony without weakening the substance of Dagestani combative techniques. Abdulmanap's capacity to explore this challenge turns into a victory that reaches out past the octagon, adding to a nuanced comprehension of how custom can coincide with development in the domain of sports.

The individual misfortune of losing his child, Abdulmanap Nurmagomedov, is a test that rises above the brandishing field, venturing into the profundities of the human experience. The less than ideal passing of Khabib sends shockwaves through the MMA people group and resonates profoundly inside the Nurmagomedov family. This significant misfortune tests Abdulmanap's flexibility, provoking him to track down importance and reason in the midst of distress. The victory over this profoundly private test turns into a demonstration of his inward strength and the persevering through tradition of his instructing reasoning.

Abdulmanap's mentorship dynamic inside the Birds MMA Club, while a wellspring of win, isn't without its difficulties. The obligation of shaping the existences of youthful competitors accompanies the heaviness of assumptions and the intricacies of self-improvement. Abdulmanap's job as a coach requires a sensitive harmony between giving direction and permitting people to explore their own ways. This mentorship challenge is an excursion set apart by the intricacies of shaping the existences of youthful competitors in a dynamic and developing games scene.

The mentorship win lies in the positive effect on the existences of his contenders. Past the triumphs in the enclosure, the getting through connections produced inside the Hawks MMA Club become a demonstration of the groundbreaking force of mentorship. Abdulmanap's mentorship goes past the specialized parts of battling; it incorporates the more extensive improvement of character, flexibility, and a feeling of obligation. The victory lies in the production of a local area that stretches out past the exercise center, where contenders become gifted competitors as well as people molded by the qualities imparted by their mentor.

In exploring these victories and difficulties, Abdulmanap Nurmagomedov's process turns into a widespread story of versatility, assurance, and the extraordinary force of sports and mentorship. His story resounds with people around the world, rising above social, geological, and disciplinary limits. Abdulmanap's story fills in as a signal, motivating others to continue on even with difficulties, safeguard social legacy, and comprehend the significant effect that mentorship can have on people and networks.

The international difficulties of Dagestan, set apart by verifiable intricacies and contemporary issues, are scenery as well as fundamental to Abdulmanap's story. The victories accomplished inside the octagon become a wellspring of pride and strength even with more extensive difficulties. Abdulmanap's training reasoning, established in the practices of Dagestani combative techniques, turns into a type of social discretion that difficulties generalizations and offers a positive story about the district.

The incorporation of customary Dagestani wrestling strategies into the universe of MMA addresses a victory over the test of safeguarding social legacy in the midst of a quickly impacting world. This combination of custom and innovation turns into a sign of Abdulmanap's instructing reasoning. The immortal viability of customary procedures becomes apparent in the outcome of his warriors, displaying that advancement inside custom can prompt victories in sports as well as in social conservation.

Abdulmanap's process is set apart by a promise to offsetting custom with development, exploring the fragile dance between saving social legacy and adjusting to the requests of the contemporary games scene. The test lies in finding some kind of harmony without weakening the substance of Dagestani combative techniques. Abdulmanap's capacity to explore this challenge turns into a victory that reaches out past the octagon, adding to a nuanced comprehension of how custom can coincide with development in the domain of sports.

The individual misfortune of losing his child, Abdulmanap Nurmagomedov, is a test that rises above the donning field, venturing into the profundities of the human experience. The less than ideal passing of Khabib sends shockwaves through the MMA people group and resonates profoundly inside the Nurmagomedov family. This significant misfortune tests Abdulmanap's flexibility, provoking him to track down importance and reason in the midst of despondency. The victory over this profoundly private test turns into a demonstration of his inward strength and the getting through tradition of his training reasoning.

Abdulmanap's mentorship dynamic inside the Birds MMA Club, while a wellspring of win, isn't without its difficulties. The obligation of shaping the existences of youthful competitors accompanies the heaviness of assumptions and the intricacies of self-awareness. Abdulmanap's job as a coach requires a fragile harmony between giving direction and permitting people to explore their own ways. This mentorship challenge is an excursion set apart by the intricacies of profoundly shaping the existences of youthful competitors in a dynamic and developing games scene.

The mentorship win lies in the positive effect on the existences of his contenders. Past the triumphs in the enclosure, the getting through connections fashioned inside the Birds MMA Club become a demonstration of the groundbreaking force of mentorship. Abdulmanap's mentorship goes past the specialized parts of battling; it includes the more extensive improvement of character, flexibility, and a feeling of obligation.

The victory lies in the making of a local area that stretches out past the rec center, where warriors become gifted competitors as well as people formed by the qualities imparted by their mentor.

In exploring these victories and difficulties, Abdulmanap Nurmagomedov's process turns into a general story of strength, assurance, and the groundbreaking force of sports and mentorship. His story resounds with people around the world, rising above social, geological, and disciplinary limits. Abdulmanap's story fills in as a signal, motivating others to drive forward notwithstanding difficulties, safeguard social legacy, and comprehend the significant effect that mentorship can have on people and networks.

Abdulmanap Nurmagomedov's story of wins and difficulties is a significant investigation of the human soul inside the setting of sports, culture, and self-improvement. His process mirrors the interconnectedness of individual encounters with more extensive international scenes, displaying the groundbreaking force of sports in molding character and rousing flexibility. Past the octagon, Abdulmanap's heritage turns into a general story that resounds across societies and disciplines, making a permanent imprint on the account of wins and difficulties in the human experience.

4.1 Analysis of key moments in Abdulmanap's coaching career, including victories and setbacks.

Abdulmanap Nurmagomedov's training vocation is an embroidery woven with the two victories and misfortunes, every second adding to the tradition of a the man job of a mentor to turn into a loved figure in the realm of blended combative techniques (MMA). Examining key minutes in Abdulmanap's training process gives experiences into the complexities of his methodology, the effect of his mentorship, and the difficulties he looked en route.

One crucial second in Abdulmanap's training vocation is the ascent of his child, Khabib Nurmagomedov, to turn into an undefeated UFC lightweight boss. The excursion to this zenith is a demonstration of Abdulmanap's instructing ability. The triumphs inside the octagon feature

Khabib's abilities as well as mirror the fastidious preparation and vital arranging ingrained by his dad. The UFC 223 title battle against Al Iaquinta stands apart as an extremely important occasion. Regardless of somewhat late rival changes, Khabib's prevailing exhibition highlighted the versatility and flexibility imparted by Abdulmanap's instructing.

The triumph at UFC 223 stamped an individual victory for Khabib as well as an approval of Abdulmanap's instructing technique. It exhibited the viability of coordinating conventional Dagestani wrestling methods into the universe of MMA, displaying that a strong groundwork in customary hand to hand fighting can be an impressive resource in the cutting edge confine. This triumph resonated past the wearing field, affecting how mentors and contenders see the collaboration among custom and development.

In any case, Abdulmanap's training process isn't without any trace of misfortunes, and one such second is the undoing of the profoundly expected session between Khabib Nurmagomedov and Tony Ferguson at UFC 249. This misfortune, brought about by the worldwide Coronavirus pandemic, was a trial of Abdulmanap's capacity to explore unexpected difficulties. The scratch-off highlighted the delicacy of plans in the realm of sports and the requirement for strength notwithstanding startling afflictions.

Abdulmanap's reaction to the mishap was normal for his realistic methodology. Instead of harping on the failure, he underlined the significance of wellbeing and security in the midst of the pandemic. This exhibited not just his obligation to the prosperity of his warriors yet additionally his capacity to keep up with viewpoint despite misfortunes. The pandemic-prompted wiping out turned into a snapshot of reflection, featuring the erratic idea of the wearing scene and the requirement for versatility in training.

One more key second in Abdulmanap's training profession is Khabib Nurmagomedov's triumph over Conor McGregor at UFC 229. The lead-up to the battle was defaced by extraordinary limited time exercises, including a profoundly broadcasted episode including the two contenders. Abdulmanap's part in keeping Khabib centered in the midst of the outside pressures became apparent. The triumph, trailed by a post-battle fight, displayed the profound and mental difficulties mentors face in dealing with their contenders, particularly in high-stakes circumstances.

Abdulmanap's reaction to the post-battle episode showed a blend of dissatisfaction and a guarantee to teach. Notwithstanding the profound power existing apart from everything else, he recognized the requirement for poise and restraint. This occurrence gave a brief look into the mind boggling elements of training in the domain of prominent, sincerely charged contests. Abdulmanap's treatment of the outcome highlighted the significance of imparting actual abilities as well as the capacity to appreciate anyone on a deeper level in his contenders.

The misfortune in the consequence of UFC 229, with both Khabib and Conor confronting suspensions and fines, turned into a vital second for Abdulmanap's training reasoning. It provoked a reexamination of the significance of discipline and sportsmanship in combative techniques. Abdulmanap's accentuation on regard, even in the intensity of contest, turned into a core value. This misfortune turned into a chance for development, molding the account of the Nurmagomedov group as talented warriors as well as people who embody the qualities imparted by their mentor.

In the midst of wins and mishaps, the heartbreaking loss of Abdulmanap Nurmagomedov himself remains as an extremely important occasion that resonated across the MMA people group. His passing denoted the conclusion of an important time period, leaving a void in the training scene. The effect of this misfortune on the warriors he guided, especially his child Khabib, was significant.

The minutes that followed, with a close to home Khabib reporting his retirement from MMA, exhibited the profound connection among mentor and contender and the significant impact Abdulmanap had on the direction of his child's profession.

The deficiency of Abdulmanap Nurmagomedov turned into a snapshot of aggregate grieving inside the MMA people group. Recognitions poured in from contenders, mentors, and fans around the world, highlighting the extensive effect of his training heritage. This second risen above the limits of the octagon, delineating how a mentor's impact stretches out past the specialized parts of battling to shape the person and character of the competitors under his direction.

In examining key minutes in Abdulmanap's training vocation, it's fundamental to dive into his training reasoning, which was instrumental in forming the stories of wins and mishaps. Fundamental to his methodology was the incorporation of customary Dagestani wrestling procedures into the preparation routine of MMA warriors. This philosophy turned into a brand name of the Nurmagomedov style, underlining the significance of a solid groundwork in customary combative techniques.

The triumphs of Khabib Nurmagomedov, especially his prevailing exhibitions on the ground, displayed the adequacy of Abdulmanap's instructing reasoning. The accentuation on wrestling, hooking, and control turned into a sign of the Nurmagomedov battling style. This approach prompted triumphs inside the enclosure as well as impacted the more extensive scene of MMA, provoking a reexamination of the significance of wrestling and hooking in contemporary blended combative techniques.

Abdulmanap's training reasoning likewise underlined the mentorship dynamic inside the Falcons MMA Club. The connection among mentor and contender was value-based as well as profoundly private. This mentorship reached out past the brandishing field, including the more extensive improvement of character, discipline, and a feeling of obligation. The snapshots of win and misfortunes became shared encounters, cementing the bonds inside the group.

One vital part of Abdulmanap's training reasoning was his obligation to social establishing. The coordination of customary Dagestani wrestling procedures was not simply a strategic decision yet an intentional work to safeguard and advance the social legacy of Dagestan. This social establishing turned into a wellspring of character and pride for the warriors under Abdulmanap's tutelage. The triumphs inside the octagon became representative of individual accomplishment as well as of the versatility and strength got from Dagestani customs.

The misfortune of the dropped session at UFC 249 because of the Coronavirus pandemic featured the weakness of even the most carefully arranged instructing techniques. Abdulmanap's reaction to this difficulty uncovered a mentor who focused on the prosperity of his contenders regardless of anything else.

The affirmation of the more extensive wellbeing worries in the midst of a worldwide pandemic exhibited a degree of obligation that went past the prompt domain of sports. This second highlighted the comprehensive methodology Abdulmanap brought to training, underlining the significance of flexibility and point of view.

Abdulmanap's training profession likewise confronted difficulties in exploring the intricacies of high-profile rivalries, as proven by the UFC 229 triumph and its result. The close to home power and outside pressures that go with such occasions request a mentor's proficient treatment of both physical and mental viewpoints. The post-battle episode and its repercussions turned into a snapshot of contemplation, provoking a reemphasis on the upsides of discipline and sportsmanship.

The unfortunate loss of Abdulmanap Nurmagomedov himself turned into a second that rose above the game. The generous flood of despondency and accolades from the MMA people group mirrored the significant effect he had on the existences of those he instructed. The story of wins and mishaps took on another aspect as contenders and fans the same wrestled with the void left by his passing. This second turned into a piercing sign of the enduring inheritance a mentor can leave and the permanent engraving they can have on the existences of their warriors.

Abdulmanap Nurmagomedov's instructing venture, a story of wins and misfortunes, is an embroidery entwined with the intricacies of mentorship, custom, and versatility. As we dive further into the key minutes that characterized his training profession, a nuanced comprehension of the man behind the triumphs and difficulties arises — a mentor whose heritage stretches out past the domain of sports.

The triumph at UFC 223, where Khabib Nurmagomedov got the lightweight title against Al Iaquinta, addresses an unparalleled accomplishment in Abdulmanap's training vocation. The versatility showed by Khabib, in spite of somewhat late changes in rivals, exhibited his ability as a contender as well as the essential splendor imparted by his dad. The victory was in excess of a particular triumph; it approved the viability of Abdulmanap's training philosophy, solidly laying out customary Dagestani wrestling methods as considerable resources in the cutting edge MMA scene.

This triumph at UFC 223 was a microcosm of Abdulmanap's instructing theory — one that consistently combined custom with development. The coordination of conventional combative techniques into the developing universe of MMA turned into a brand name of the Nurmagomedov style, testing assumptions about the fundamental range of abilities for outcome in the octagon. The meaning of this win stretches out past private honors; it reshaped the talk around preparing systems in blended hand to hand fighting.

Be that as it may, as Abdulmanap directed his warriors to wins, the capricious idea of the donning scene introduced its own arrangement of difficulties. The crossing out of the exceptionally expected session among Khabib and Tony Ferguson at UFC 249 because of the Coronavirus pandemic was a distinct sign of the delicacy of plans even with outside powers. The pandemic-prompted misfortune turned into a trial of Abdulmanap's flexibility and versatility, underscoring the requirement for mentors to explore unexpected difficulties with self-restraint and vital premonition.

Abdulmanap's reaction to the difficulty exemplified a mentor who focused on the security and prosperity of his warriors regardless of anything else. As opposed to surrendering to disillusionment, he embraced the more extensive wellbeing concerns presented by the pandemic, exhibiting a point of view that stretched out past the quick domain of sports. This snapshot of difficulty turned into a chance for reflection, featuring the all encompassing methodology Abdulmanap brought to training — a methodology grounded in liability and a significant comprehension of the interconnectedness of sports with more extensive cultural difficulties.

One more vital second in Abdulmanap's training process was Khabib's triumph over Conor McGregor at UFC 229. The lead-up to the battle was damaged by extreme limited time exercises and a profoundly broadcasted episode including the two warriors. Abdulmanap's job in keeping Khabib centered in the midst of the outside pressures turned into a demonstration of the profound and mental difficulties mentors face in dealing with their contenders, particularly in high-stakes circumstances.

The triumph over McGregor, trailed by a post-battle fight, highlighted the close to home power innate in high-profile rivalries. Abdulmanap's reaction to the post-battle episode showed a mix of disillusionment and a promise to teach. Notwithstanding the turbulent fallout, his accentuation on levelheadedness and poise displayed the more extensive illustrations imparted in his contenders past simple actual abilities. The mishaps and discussions became open doors for Abdulmanap to build up the upsides of regard and sportsmanship — a demonstration of the profundity of his training reasoning.

In looking at Abdulmanap's training vocation, the terrible loss of the mentor himself remains as a permanent second that rises above the wearing field. His passing denoted the conclusion of an important time period, leaving an indispensable void in the realm of MMA training. The effect of this misfortune on the contenders he guided, especially his child Khabib, was significant. The minutes that followed, with a close to home Khabib reporting his retirement from MMA, exhibited the profound connection among mentor and contender and the significant impact Abdulmanap had on the direction of his child's profession.

The deficiency of Abdulmanap Nurmagomedov turned into a snapshot of aggregate grieving inside the MMA people group. Accolades poured in from warriors, mentors, and fans around the world, mirroring the sweeping effect of his training heritage. This second risen above the bounds of the octagon, showing how a mentor's impact reaches out past the specialized parts of battling to shape the person and character of the competitors under his direction.

The examination of key minutes in Abdulmanap's training profession uncovers a mentor whose heritage goes past the quantity of triumphs his warriors gathered. His training reasoning, secured in customary Dagestani hand to hand fighting, turned into a worldview for progress in the cutting edge universe of blended combative techniques. The triumphs inside the octagon became emblematic of individual accomplishment as well as of the more extensive social pride and strength got from Dagestani customs.

Mishaps, whether as dropped sessions or post-battle discussions, became extraordinary minutes for development and reflection. Abdulmanap's reactions to these difficulties exhibited his strategic keenness as well as his obligation to the prosperity, discipline, and social establishing of his contenders. The terrible loss of Abdulmanap himself turned into a second that rose above the game, featuring the getting through influence a mentor can have on the existences of those they guide.

Abdulmanap Nurmagomedov's training process, set apart by wins and misfortunes, is a demonstration of the getting through impact of a the mentor limits of the wearing field. His inheritance lives on in the triumphs inside the octagon as well as in the qualities imparted in the contenders he guided and the more extensive effect on the scene of blended combative techniques. In the account of Abdulmanap's training vocation, the triumphs and misfortunes are not simple achievements but rather parts in a story that keeps on resounding with contenders, fans, and mentors the same — an account of custom, strength, and the enduring engraving of an unbelievable mentor.

4.2 Personal struggles and how he navigated challenges in the pursuit of excellence.

Abdulmanap Nurmagomedov's excursion, set apart by private battles and wins, discloses a story of versatility, assurance, and the resolute quest for greatness. To grasp the profundity of his personality and the difficulties he explored, one should dive into the individual parts of his life — an excursion that molded the man as well as the mentor whose impact reached out a long ways past the limits of the octagon.

Brought into the world in Sildi, a distant town in Dagestan, Abdulmanap experienced childhood in a district set apart by its international intricacies and verifiable difficulties. Dagestan, situated at the junction of Eastern Europe and Western Asia, has a rich social embroidery woven with different nationalities and a set of experiences molded by the recurring pattern of realms.

The international difficulties of the district turned into a natural piece of Abdulmanap's initial life, impacting his viewpoint and ingraining a feeling of flexibility that would characterize his excursion.

Chasing greatness, Abdulmanap confronted the difficulties inborn in a district set apart by monetary differences and restricted open doors. The rough landscape of Dagestan, while pleasant, presented hindrances to individual and expert turn of events. The shortage of assets, combined with the requests of a difficult climate, required a tireless soul — one that Abdulmanap encapsulated since early on.

Abdulmanap's own battles were formed by outside factors as well as were additionally profoundly interlaced with the social texture of Dagestan. As a young fellow drenched in the customs of his country, he wrestled with the assumptions set upon him by cultural standards. The heaviness of familial and cultural assumptions turned into a cauldron wherein his personality was produced. This unseen conflict, intrinsic chasing individual and expert greatness, established the groundwork for the versatility that would turn into a sign of his training reasoning.

The quest for greatness drove Abdulmanap to drench himself in the realm of combative techniques, especially the conventional Dagestani wrestling known as "Khapsagay." This old type of wrestling, well established in the social legacy of the district, became both an actual discipline and an otherworldly pursuit for Abdulmanap. The preparation grounds, frequently without current conveniences, turned into the cauldron where he improved his wrestling abilities as well as his psychological determination — a strength that would later be granted to the contenders he instructed.

Abdulmanap's initial a long time as a competitor were set apart by the double difficulties of dominating his specialty and exploring the intricacies of life in Dagestan. The thorough instructional meetings, frequently directed in unforgiving circumstances, imparted in him a discipline that rose above the bounds of the wrestling mat. These early battles were physical as well as mental, requesting a degree of mental flexibility that would later turn into a characterizing component of his training reasoning.

The difficulties looked by Abdulmanap stretched out past the domain of sports. As a young fellow with yearnings past the limits of his town, he experienced cultural assumptions that looked to characterize his way. The customary standards of Dagestani society, while wealthy in social legacy, now and again conflicted with the yearnings of people looking to break liberated from ordinary jobs. Abdulmanap's process turned into a sensitive dance between protecting social character and chasing after private greatness — a battle that reflected the more extensive elements of a locale exploring custom and innovation.

In his quest for greatness, Abdulmanap's process took him to the renowned Makhachkala Foundation of Actual Culture, where he further improved his wrestling abilities and developed how he might interpret sports science. The scholastic pursuit resembled his obligation to the actual parts of his specialty, making a comprehensive way to deal with preparing that would later characterize his instructing strategy. The combination of conventional wrestling strategies with current games science turned into a foundation of Abdulmanap's training reasoning — a way of thinking that looked to wed the immortal insight of

Dagestani combative techniques with the headways of the contemporary games scene.

As he left on his training vocation, Abdulmanap confronted the test of exploring a mind boggling scene where custom and development frequently remained in conflict. The universe of blended hand to hand fighting, actually developing and tracking down its place inside the more extensive games local area, introduced novel difficulties and valuable open doors. Abdulmanap's obligation to saving the social legacy of Dagestan turned into a core value, molding the manner in which he moved toward the preparation and improvement of his warriors.

The individual battles of Abdulmanap stretched out to the intricacies of everyday life. Adjusting the requests of a training vocation with the obligations of parenthood made a unique in which individual and expert circles crossed. The assumptions put upon him as a dad and a mentor were many-sided strings in the embroidery of his life. Sustaining the yearnings of his child, Khabib Nurmagomedov, added an extra layer of intricacy to Abdulmanap's excursion.

The intricacies of parenthood and training arrived at an impactful crossroads with the terrible loss of Abdulmanap's child, Vismail, in a fender bender. The misery and distress that went with this significant misfortune tried Abdulmanap's strength in manners that rose above the difficulties of sports. The profoundly private battle turned into a pot where he faced the delicacy of life and the intricacies of human feelings. This experience, while covered in misfortune, added an element of sympathy and understanding to Abdulmanap's training, building up the significance of mentorship past the specialized parts of battling.

Exploring individual battles expected Abdulmanap to draw upon a wellspring of inward strength, otherworldliness, and the social establishing of Dagestan. His confidence, well established in the practices of Islam, gave a wellspring of comfort and direction during testing times. The profound components of his process became basic to the account, molding his own standpoint as well as affecting the manner in which he conferred values to the contenders under his tutelage.

The story of individual battles and wins in Abdulmanap's day to day existence is indistinguishable from the more extensive setting of Dagestan — a locale set apart by a mosaic of nationalities, dialects, and social customs. The international difficulties that characterized Dagestan's set of experiences turned into an inherent piece of Abdulmanap's personality.

The cultural assumptions, the financial difficulties, and the conflict among custom and advancement became cauldrons in which his personality was tempered.

As Abdulmanap rose to unmistakable quality as a mentor, the difficulties of exploring the developing scene of blended hand to hand fighting introduced the two snags and open doors. The conflict among custom and development, combined with the requests of high-profile rivalries, expected a mentor to adjust while remaining consistent with the social roots that characterized him. Abdulmanap's process turned into a sensitive dance, a nuanced discussion between saving social character and embracing the dynamism of the brandishing scene.

In confronting individual battles, Abdulmanap's process procured a widespread reverberation. His story, while well established in the social particulars of Dagestan, turned into a demonstration of the human experience — set apart by versatility, assurance, and the extraordinary force of sports and mentorship. The battles were not segregated occurrences but rather strings woven into the bigger embroidery of his life, making a story that rises above the octagon and reverberates with people exploring their own ways.

The awfulness of losing his child, Vismail, filled in as a pot that tried Abdulmanap's personality and flexibility. The significant despondency and distress turned into a profoundly private battle, one that necessary close to home determination as well as a reconsideration of life's needs. The convergence of individual misfortune with the requests of training made a powerful second in Abdulmanap's excursion — one that featured the human components of a his mentor, regardless of his job in forming champions, wrestled with similar weaknesses as any dad or tutor.

Abdulmanap's instructing reasoning, molded by private battles, mirrors a pledge to mentorship that goes past the specialized parts of battling. His methodology is saturated with compassion, understanding, and an acknowledgment of the more extensive human experience. The examples drawn from individual victories and misfortunes become the core values that illuminate his mentorship, making a unique wherein contenders are competitors as well as people exploring the intricacies of life.

The profound elements of Abdulmanap's excursion, well established in the customs of Islam, add a layer of intricacy to the story of individual battles. His confidence, a wellspring of solidarity and comfort, turns into a directing power that shapes his point of view and impacts the manner in which he gives values to his contenders. The convergence of otherworldliness with the actual requests of training makes an all encompassing methodology — one that perceives the interconnectedness of brain, body, and soul.

Abdulmanap's process unfurls as a story of a singular looking for greatness amidst individual and cultural difficulties. The intricacies of life in Dagestan, the requests of training in the developing universe of blended hand to hand fighting, and the profoundly private battles of parenthood and misfortune join to make a rich embroidery of encounters. His story turns into a demonstration of the strength that rises up out of exploring the crossing point of individual and expert circles — a flexibility that turns into a guide for those wrestling with their own battles.

Chasing greatness, Abdulmanap Nurmagomedov's process turns into an investigation of the human soul — a soul that rises above the limits of culture, geology, and game. His story is a demonstration of the extraordinary force of individual battles, forming the mentor as well as the guide whose impact stretches out past the octagon. The difficulties he confronted, while profoundly private, become general touchpoints for people looking for motivation and versatility on their own excursions. In Abdulmanap's story, individual battles are not obstructions but rather basic components that add to the wealth of a day to day existence lived with reason and devotion.

4.3 Examination of his resilience and determination.

Abdulmanap Nurmagomedov's biography is a remarkable demonstration of versatility and assurance, characteristics that have characterized his excursion from a youthful Dagestani kid with dreams to perhaps of the most worshipped mentor in the realm of blended combative techniques (MMA). His strength isn't only a reaction to challenges however a fundamental component that formed his personality, his instructing reasoning, and the permanent inheritance he abandons.

Naturally introduced to the rough scenes of Dagestan, Abdulmanap's initial years were set apart by the difficulties inborn in a locale with a mind boggling history and a mix of social impacts. The international complexities of Dagestan, arranged at the junction of Eastern Europe and Western Asia, added to a climate where versatility wasn't simply a goodness yet a need. The monetary variations and restricted open doors presented impressive obstructions that Abdulmanap, even in his childhood, faced with a relentless assurance to rise above limits.

His assurance to transcend conditions showed right off the bat in his obligation to hand to hand fighting, especially the customary Dagestani wrestling known as "Khapsagay." The quest for greatness in a game profoundly implanted in the social texture of Dagestan turned into a vehicle for Abdulmanap to channel his assurance. Wrestling, a genuinely requesting discipline. required expertise as well as a dauntless will — a will produced in the cauldron of Dagestan's difficult landscape and intelligent of a versatility that would later characterize his training vocation.

Abdulmanap's excursion into the universe of wrestling wasn't simply a special goal; it was a pathway to rise above the limits forced by cultural assumptions and financial difficulties.

The wrestling mat turned into a material where his assurance painted a story of self-awareness, expertise improvement, and the unfaltering purpose to cut out an alternate direction for himself. The examples mastered during these early stages laid the preparation for the instructing reasoning that would later shape the professions of his contenders.

The quest for greatness, frequently joined by private penances, drove Abdulmanap to the Makhachkala Establishment of Actual Culture. This scholarly pursuit, related to his proceeded with devotion to wrestling, denoted a stage in which assurance tracked down articulation in actual preparation as well as in scholarly development. The combination of conventional wrestling strategies with a more profound comprehension of sports science turned into a demonstration of his assurance to develop and adjust, a rule that would later characterize his instructing procedure.

As Abdulmanap changed into a training job, his assurance confronted new difficulties in the quickly developing universe of MMA. The conflict among custom and development, the requests of high-profile contests, and the intricacies of overseeing warriors expected a mentor with an unfaltering obligation to his standards. Abdulmanap's assurance to save the social legacy of Dagestan while embracing the dynamism of the brandishing scene turned into a sensitive difficult exercise — a demonstration of a strength established in social pride.

The individual battles that obvious Abdulmanap's excursion, including the deficiency of his child Vismail, delivered an alternate component of his assurance. Despondency and distress, significant and individual, turned into extra obstacles that requested a novel type of versatility. The assurance to explore these difficulties without surrendering to surrender displayed the mentor's grit as well as the profundity of his mankind. Notwithstanding such significant misfortune, Abdulmanap's assurance turned into a wellspring of motivation for people around him, representing that even in the most obscure minutes, one can track down the solidarity to continue on.

The otherworldly elements of Abdulmanap's assurance can't be put into words. Established in the practices of Islam, his confidence gave an ethical compass as well as a wellspring of internal strength during testing times. The crossing point of otherworldliness with the actual requests of instructing made a comprehensive methodology — one where assurance drew from a wellspring that rose above the physical and the material. This interchange among confidence and assurance became fundamental to the account of his instructing reasoning, affecting his way to deal with the game as well as the manner in which he conferred values to his warriors.

The strength of Abdulmanap Nurmagomedov tracked down a significant articulation in his capacity to explore the difficulties presented by cultural assumptions. As a young fellow looking to break liberated from customary jobs, he wrestled with the conflict between conventional standards and individual yearnings.

The assurance to seek after a way past the normal direction uncovered a strength that was physical as well as a relentless obligation to individual independence. Abdulmanap's excursion, in such manner, became meaningful of the more extensive cultural movements and the elements of social advancement in Dagestan.

Abdulmanap's assurance to adjust the requests of everyday existence with the afflictions of training added one more layer to his story. The intricacies of parenthood, especially in a culture that puts critical significance on familial obligations, required a versatility that reached out past the limits of the rec center. Sustaining the yearnings of his child, Khabib Nurmagomedov, while dealing with the difficulties presented by cultural assumptions requested a fragile dance — a dance that Abdulmanap executed with an assurance to give the most ideal direction to his family and contenders.

The assurance of Abdulmanap confronted one of its most imposing tests with the appalling loss of his child, Vismail. The sadness that followed might have been an unrealistic obstacle, at this point Abdulmanap's flexibility radiated through. The assurance to channel this significant misfortune into a wellspring of motivation for him as well as his contenders highlighted a flexibility that rose above private misfortune. Instead of capitulating to surrender, Abdulmanap figured out how to change distress into an impetus for individual and aggregate development.

As a mentor, Abdulmanap's assurance appeared in the careful preparation regimens, the essential preparation, and the immovable obligation to the progress of his contenders. The triumphs inside the octagon weren't simply a consequence of specialized ability however an impression of the assurance imparted by their mentor. The reconciliation of customary Dagestani wrestling procedures, combined with a cutting edge comprehension of sports science, displayed an assurance to develop and enhance — a responsibility that added to the outcome of his warriors on the worldwide stage.

The assurance showed by Abdulmanap during the scratch-off of the profoundly expected session among Khabib and Tony Ferguson at UFC 249 because of the Coronavirus pandemic is important. The mishap, however frustrating, turned into a chance for Abdulmanap to show flexibility and an emphasis on the prosperity of his contenders. Rather than harping on the difficulties presented by the pandemic, he underlined the more extensive wellbeing concerns, displaying an assurance that focused on liability over quick donning desires.

The difficulties introduced by the developing scene of MMA, including high-profile contests and special tensions, requested a mentor with an undaunted assurance to keep up with discipline and maintain values. Abdulmanap's reaction to the post-battle occurrence following Khabib's triumph over Conor McGregor at UFC 229 exemplified this versatility. The mistake in the consequence of the episode was met with an assurance to stress the significance of poise and restraint, supporting the upsides of regard and sportsmanship.

Abdulmanap's assurance to save the social legacy of Dagestan, especially through the advancement of customary hand to hand fighting, turned into a particular element of his training reasoning. The conflict between protecting practice and embracing development in the realm of MMA expected a mentor with the versatility to explore this fragile equilibrium. Abdulmanap's obligation to coordinating customary Dagestani wrestling procedures, even despite developing preparation strategies, exhibited an assurance that went past regular standards.

The triumphs got by his contenders, especially Khabib's predominance in the lightweight division, are a demonstration of the assurance imparted by Abdulmanap. His training reasoning, secured in the standards of conventional Dagestani hand to hand fighting, turned into a worldview for outcome in the cutting edge universe of MMA. The victories inside the octagon celebrated individual triumphs as well as mirrored the more extensive social pride and flexibility got from Dagestani customs.

Abdulmanap's flexibility and assurance arrived at their zenith during his child's transient ascent to turning into the UFC lightweight hero. The difficulties confronted, both inside and outside the octagon, requested a mentor with a steady assurance to direct his warrior through the turbulent excursion of expert MMA. Khabib's undefeated record and his predominance in the lightweight division reflected the assurance imparted by his dad — an assurance that rose above the game and turned into an image of Dagestani pride.

The awfulness of Abdulmanap's passing in 2020 denoted a significant second where strength met its definitive test. The void left by his takeoff, both in the existences of his contenders and the more extensive MMA people group, was a distinct sign of the effect a mentor can have. The assurance Abdulmanap showed in beating individual battles, exploring cultural assumptions, and molding the professions of his contenders turned into a heritage that rose above his actual presence.

The assessment of Abdulmanap Nurmagomedov's flexibility and assurance uncovers a day to day existence story set apart by wins, difficulties, and a resolute obligation to greatness. From the moving scenes of Dagestan to the worldwide phase of MMA, his assurance turned into the main impetus behind private and expert achievement. The strength showed even with individual misfortunes and cultural assumptions exhibited a mentor whose impact stretched out past the limits of the octagon.

The assurance to save the social legacy of Dagestan, coordinate customary combative techniques with current preparation systems, and guide his warriors to triumph on the worldwide stage characterized Abdulmanap's training reasoning. The triumphs inside the octagon were about individual accomplishment as well as mirrored a more extensive story of social pride and strength. The awfulness of Abdulmanap's passing underscored the persevering through tradition of a mentor whose assurance keeps on motivating warriors, mentors, and fans around the world.

Abdulmanap Nurmagomedov's biography is a demonstration of the groundbreaking force of assurance — a power that shapes individual fates as well as makes a permanent imprint on the more extensive embroidery of sports and social personality. His heritage, established in the upsides of flexibility and obligation to greatness, fills in as a wellspring of motivation for a long time into the future.

Chapter 5

Legacy Beyond the Gym

Abdulmanap Nurmagomedov's inheritance reaches out a long ways past the bounds of the rec center and the universe of blended combative techniques (MMA). His effect on the Dagestani people group, the more extensive games scene, and the advancement of solid ways of life epitomize a heritage that rises above the accomplishments inside the octagon. Abdulmanap's commitments to local area improvement, his obligation to schooling, and his promotion for solid living address a complex heritage that reflects the mentor as well as the man committed to having a constructive outcome in the existences of everyone around him.

One of the critical features of Abdulmanap's heritage is his part in local area advancement inside Dagestan. Brought into the world in Sildi, a distant town in the republic, Abdulmanap comprehended the difficulties looked by the nearby populace. His assurance to reward his local area became clear as he rose to noticeable quality in the realm of MMA. As opposed to being bound to the marvelousness and style of the battling field, Abdulmanap kept a profound association with his underlying foundations, underscoring the significance of local area commitment.

Abdulmanap's drives in local area improvement were different and significant. From coordinating wrestling competitions to laying out preparing offices in far off towns, he tried to give open doors to the nearby youth to decidedly channel their energies. These endeavors weren't just about delivering future contenders however making a feeling of local area pride and encouraging discipline among the young. Abdulmanap's heritage, in such manner, is entwined with the upliftment of Dagestan's grassroots, making a gradually expanding influence that reached out past the universe of sports.

Instruction was one more mainstay of Abdulmanap's heritage past the exercise center. Perceiving the groundbreaking force of information, he effectively upheld instructive drives in Dagestan. Whether through grants for promising understudies or by advancing the significance of scholastic pursuits close by athletic undertakings, Abdulmanap tried to make an all encompassing way to deal with improvement. His confidence in the advantageous connection among scholarly and actual development resounded with the more extensive cultural yearnings of Dagestan.

Abdulmanap's obligation to instruction was tied in with encouraging scholastic greatness as well as imparting upsides of discipline, obligation, and social pride. By stressing the significance of instruction close by hand to hand fighting preparation, he intended to create balanced people who could contribute definitively to society. The tradition of schooling entwined with Abdulmanap's name mirrors a mentor who comprehended the more extensive job he played in molding the eventual fate of Dagestan.

The advancement of solid ways of life arose as one more critical part of Abdulmanap's heritage. In a locale where monetary difficulties and restricted admittance to assets presented hindrances to prosperity, he turned into a backer for actual wellness and sound residing. His instructing reasoning reached out past the rec center, accentuating the significance of sustenance, work out, and mental prosperity. Abdulmanap's heritage in advancing sound ways of life isn't just found in the actual changes of his warriors yet in addition in the more extensive local area's consciousness of the significance of prosperity.

Through open mindfulness crusades, work out regimes, and commitment with neighborhood wellbeing drives, Abdulmanap turned into a main thrust behind a social shift toward better living in Dagestan. The tradition of advancing wellbeing and wellness mirrors a mentor who comprehended that the effect of his work went past the quick triumphs in the octagon. It stretched out to making a better, stronger local area that could defeat the difficulties presented by financial variables and international intricacies.

The social pride implanted in Abdulmanap's training reasoning tracked down articulation in his endeavors to save and advance conventional Dagestani combative techniques. Past the rec center, he turned into an overseer of the rich social legacy of Dagestan, guaranteeing that the conventional wrestling strategies and values were passed down to people in the future.

This obligation to social safeguarding turned into a foundation of his heritage, supporting that progress in the donning field was unpredictably connected to a significant feeling of social character.

Abdulmanap's effect on social protection went past hypothetical backing. His drives incorporated the foundation of preparing fixates that zeroed in on customary Dagestani wrestling. These focuses filled in as centers for athletic improvement as well as stores of social information. The tradition of social protection exemplified by Abdulmanap is a demonstration of a that mentor progress in sports was not a takeoff from social roots but rather a confirmation of them.

The worldwide progress of warriors prepared under Abdulmanap's direction turned into a wellspring of pride for Dagestan and the bigger North Caucasus district. His heritage, hence, became interlaced with the district's character, representing versatility, discipline, and a relentless obligation to greatness. The effect arrived at past public boundaries, as warriors like Khabib Nurmagomedov became worldwide representatives for Dagestani hand to hand fighting and culture.

Abdulmanap's heritage is likewise set apart by his job as a tutor and mentor to numerous in the MMA people group. His impact reached out past the contenders he straightforwardly trained, including a more extensive organization of competitors who admired him for direction. The regard and adoration he collected from contenders across various exercise centers and trains highlighted the profundity of his effect. Abdulmanap's heritage as a guide reverberates with the possibility that training goes past specialized guidance — it includes forming character, imparting values, and offering unfaltering help.

The disastrous loss of Abdulmanap in 2020 resounded in the MMA people group as well as among his various admirers and devotees. The aggregate grieving that followed featured the significant effect he had on the existences of those he contacted. Recognitions poured in from warriors, mentors, and fans around the world, representing the worldwide reach of his heritage. Abdulmanap's passing turned into a snapshot of reflection for the MMA people group, inciting a more profound appreciation for the commitments he made to the game and the lives he impacted.

Abdulmanap Nurmagomedov's inheritance past the rec center is an embroidery woven with strings of local area improvement, training, advancement of solid ways of life, social protection, and mentorship. His effect on Dagestan, the more extensive MMA scene, and the worldwide impression of Dagestani combative techniques is significant. Abdulmanap's inheritance isn't bound to triumphs to the octagon; a living demonstration of a mentor comprehended that his impact arrived at a long ways past the rec center walls. The persevering through effect of his work mirrors a promise to greatness that reaches out past the quick domain of sports, making a permanent imprint on the social, instructive, and wellbeing scene of Dagestan and then some.

5.1 Abdulmanap's influence on the cultural and social landscape of Dagestan and beyond.

Abdulmanap Nurmagomedov's impact on the social and social scene of Dagestan rises above the domains of sports, venturing profound into the core of a locale with a rich embroidery of customs, identities, and narratives. His inheritance isn't restricted to the triumphs accomplished inside the octagon however reaches out to the actual texture of Dagestani personality. The impact of Abdulmanap on the social and social scene is a complex story, intertwined with his obligation to protecting practice, encouraging solidarity, and moving ages.

At its center, Abdulmanap's effect on Dagestani culture is attached in his commitment to customary hand to hand fighting. Dagestan, with its different ethnic gatherings and verifiable intricacies, has a well established custom of wrestling and combative techniques. Abdulmanap, brought into the world in the town of Sildi, drenched himself in this social legacy since early on. His excursion from a neighborhood wrestling lover to a worldwide perceived mentor reflects the more extensive story of Dagestan — a locale where the reverberations of old practices mix with the elements of innovation.

Abdulmanap's obligation to customary Dagestani wrestling, frequently alluded to as "Khapsagay," goes past the specialized parts of the game. It typifies a social conservation exertion — a cognizant choice to shield the unmistakable military fine arts that have been gone down through ages. In laying out preparing focuses and advancing the significance of these customary procedures, Abdulmanap turned into an overseer of Dagestani social legacy.

The impact on Dagestani culture is likewise clear in Abdulmanap's job as a tutor to youthful contenders. Past giving specialized abilities, he ingrained upsides of discipline, regard, and social pride. His instructing reasoning was a mix of revered customs and present day preparing strategies — a combination that resounded with the developing yearnings of Dagestani youth. The effect of his mentorship reaches out past the rec center, molding the personality of people who lead of Dagestani hand to hand fighting.

The solidarity cultivated by Abdulmanap in Dagestan is a pivotal part of his social impact. Dagestan, with its mosaic of nationalities and dialects, has generally confronted difficulties connected with character and regionalism. Abdulmanap's training reasoning, underlining a typical social legacy, gave a binding together story. Warriors from various ethnic foundations prepared next to each other, joined by a common obligation to greatness and an aggregate pride in their Dagestani character.

The solidarity reached out past the rec center, making a feeling of kinship and fortitude among Dagestanis.

Abdulmanap's impact, hence, isn't simply in the triumphs accomplished by individual warriors however in the encouraging of an aggregate soul that rises above ethnic and local divisions. His heritage is entwined with the possibility that Dagestan's solidarity lies in its solidarity — an idea that resounds profoundly in a locale set apart by its variety.

Abdulmanap's effect on the social scene of Dagestan is likewise reflected in his drives for local area improvement. Perceiving the difficulties looked by his kindred Dagestanis, particularly those in far off towns, he found a way unmistakable ways to give open doors. From coordinating wrestling competitions in nearby networks to laying out preparing offices in less advantaged regions, Abdulmanap's commitments tended to financial differences. The tradition of local area improvement reaches out to engaging the young, offering them a pathway to progress past the limitations of their nearby conditions.

The accentuation on training inside Abdulmanap's instructing reasoning is one more element of his effect on the social scene. In a locale where admittance to quality schooling can be restricted, Abdulmanap effectively upheld instructive drives. Grants for promising understudies and support for scholastic pursuits close by athletic preparation highlighted his confidence in the groundbreaking force of information. Abdulmanap's heritage, in such manner, isn't just about creating gifted warriors yet supporting taught people who can contribute definitively to Dagestani society.

The social effect of Abdulmanap's impact is maybe most substantial in the more extensive acknowledgment and pride that Dagestanis feel in their social accomplishments. His job in molding warriors who became worldwide symbols raised the perceivability of Dagestani combative techniques on the global stage. This acknowledgment imparted a feeling of satisfaction and personality among Dagestanis, who found a wellspring of motivation in the examples of overcoming adversity of warriors like Khabib Nurmagomedov. Abdulmanap's heritage, hence, added to a positive change in the social view of Dagestan, featuring its social lavishness and athletic ability.

The effect on Dagestani culture likewise reaches out to the more extensive North Caucasus locale, where shared narratives and interconnected personalities make a feeling of territorial fortitude. Abdulmanap's instructing achievement turned into a wellspring of territorial pride, moving yearnings past Dagestan's boundaries. The social trade worked with by Abdulmanap's drives, including worldwide instructional courses and coordinated efforts, advanced the more extensive social scene of the North Caucasus. The tradition of multifaceted commitment underlines his vision of Dagestan as an essential piece of a bigger provincial embroidery.

Abdulmanap's impact on the social and social scene isn't without any trace of difficulties and intricacies. Dagestan, in the same way as other districts with a rich social legacy, wrestles with the powerful transaction among custom and advancement. Abdulmanap explored these intricacies by taking on a methodology that regarded custom while embracing development.

The combination of customary Dagestani wrestling procedures with current games science exhibited a nuanced comprehension of the requirement for variation without compromising social genuineness.

The grievous loss of Abdulmanap in 2020 denoted an impactful second in the social and social scene of Dagestan. The aggregate sorrow and grieving that followed represented the profundity of his effect. The flood of accolades, from the MMA people group as well as from Dagestanis across different backgrounds, featured the significant and persevering through impact he had on the district's social character. The void left by his passing turned into a snapshot of reflection, provoking a reestablished appreciation for the social inheritance he abandons.

Abdulmanap Nurmagomedov's impact on the social and social scene of Dagestan kept on developing, making a permanent imprint on the district's direction. His effect wasn't restricted to a solitary aspect; rather, it resonated through different features, molding the manner in which Dagestanis see their personality, draw in with custom, and imagine their aggregate future.

One of the persevering through traditions of Abdulmanap is the strengthening of Dagestani youth through sports. By laying out preparing focuses and arranging wrestling competitions in nearby networks, he gave a road to youthful gifts to usefully channel their energies. This grassroots way to deal with sports developed future warriors as well as imparted upsides of discipline, cooperation, and flexibility among the adolescent. Abdulmanap's impact, hence, should be visible as an impetus for supporting an age that perspectives sports as a serious field as well as a vehicle for self-awareness and local area improvement.

The feeling of solidarity cultivated by Abdulmanap took on a more profound importance against the setting of verifiable and international intricacies in Dagestan. The area, portrayed by its different ethnic gatherings and etymological variety, has wrestled with difficulties connected with character and regionalism. Abdulmanap's training reasoning, which united contenders from various ethnic foundations under a typical flag of Dagestani pride, turned into a bringing together power. In the rec center, qualifications obscured, and an aggregate character arose that rose above ethnic and phonetic partitions. This solidarity, sustained by Abdulmanap, holds the possibility to add to a more durable and amicable social texture in Dagestan.

The effect on the social scene is additionally exemplified by Abdulmanap's promotion for training. In a district where instructive open doors can be restricted, his accentuation on the harmonious connection between scholastic pursuits and athletic preparation turned into a core value. Grants for promising understudies and support for contenders to seek after instruction close by sports highlighted his obligation to comprehensive turn of events. The tradition of Abdulmanap, in this specific circumstance, becomes entwined with the instructive yearnings of Dagestani youth, offering them a pathway to progress that envelops both scholarly and actual greatness.

The social protection endeavors drove by Abdulmanap showed in preparing focuses as well as in his dynamic advancement of customary Dagestani wrestling methods. This obligation to safeguarding the unmistakable military artistic expressions went down through ages guaranteed that the rich social legacy of Dagestan stayed dynamic and important. By coordinating these conventional procedures with current games science, Abdulmanap exhibited a nuanced way to deal with social conservation — one that perceives the requirement for variation while shielding the embodiment of custom. This heritage turns into a social extension, interfacing the past with the present and guaranteeing the progression of Dagestan's hand to hand fighting inheritance.

The global acknowledgment collected by contenders prepared under Abdulmanap turned into a wellspring of pride for Dagestan as well as for the more extensive North Caucasus district. The examples of overcoming adversity of warriors like Khabib Nurmagomedov raised the worldwide impression of Dagestani combative techniques, exhibiting the locale as a force to be reckoned with of ability and strength. Abdulmanap's impact, hence, stretches out past provincial boundaries, adding to a positive story about the North Caucasus that goes past verifiable generalizations.

Abdulmanap's impact on the social and social scene likewise includes the fragile harmony among custom and innovation. Dagestan, in the same way as other districts with a rich social history, faces the test of exploring social safeguarding in the midst of the powers of globalization and cultural change. Abdulmanap's methodology, which embraces custom while consolidating present day preparing procedures, turns into a model for exploring this complicated landscape. His heritage mirrors a unique comprehension that custom can be a wellspring of solidarity, giving an establishment to flexibility and personality, even notwithstanding developing cultural elements.

The grievous loss of Abdulmanap in 2020 denoted a piercing part in the social and social scene of Dagestan. The aggregate grieving that followed highlighted the significant effect he had on the existences of Dagestanis. The void left by his takeoff turned into a material whereupon the aggregate appreciation for his commitments to social protection, local area improvement, and personality development was painted. The despondency communicated was for the passing of a mentor as well as for a social symbol whose impact arrived at a long ways past the domains of sports.

The continuous effect of Abdulmanap's heritage is obvious in the proceeded with progress of contenders from Dagestan on the worldwide stage. The torchbearers of his training reasoning, who keep on rivaling differentiation, act as living epitomes of the standards he ingrained. Their accomplishments add to a continuous account of Dagestani strength and greatness, supporting the getting through impact of Abdulmanap on the social and social scene.

Abdulmanap Nurmagomedov's impact on the social and social scene of Dagestan is an account of strengthening, solidarity, instruction, and social protection. His inheritance stretches out past the rec center, forming the manner in which Dagestanis see their character and draw in with their social legacy. Abdulmanap's effect is a demonstration of the groundbreaking influence of sports, schooling, and social pride — an inheritance that keeps on developing, moving ages and making a permanent imprint on the rich embroidery of Dagestani society.

5.2 Recognition of his efforts in promoting discipline, respect, and unity.

Abdulmanap Nurmagomedov's endeavors in advancing discipline, regard, and solidarity stand as mainstays of his training reasoning, contributing not exclusively to the progress of his contenders yet in addition making a persevering through imprint on the more extensive scene of blended combative techniques (MMA). His obligation to imparting these qualities goes past the specialized parts of preparing; it mirrors a significant comprehension that the pith of a military craftsman reaches out past the limits of the octagon.

Discipline, in Abdulmanap's training reasoning, is a foundation that shapes the bedrock of progress. Conceived out of his own encounters in Dagestan, where financial difficulties and cultural assumptions could undoubtedly get sidetracked, discipline turned into a core value. The afflictions of Dagestani wrestling, profoundly imbued in the social texture, gave Abdulmanap an establishment whereupon to construct talented warriors as well as people with a restrained way to deal with life.

Discipline in Abdulmanap's instructing is definitely not a simple adherence to preparing plans and actual schedules; it stretches out to the development of mental strength and close to home versatility. Contenders under his direction are ingrained with a feeling of obligation and commitment that rises above the bounds of the rec center. The examples learned through focused preparing become a microcosm of life's difficulties, getting ready warriors for triumph inside the octagon as well as for the more extensive excursion of individual and expert development.

Regard is one more key worth advanced by Abdulmanap, intelligent of the social ethos of Dagestan. In a game frequently portrayed by extreme competitions and pre-battle vain behaviors, Abdulmanap's accentuation on regard turns into a distinctive element. Regard, in his training reasoning, is diverse — it stretches out to adversaries, mentors, authorities, and the actual game. This ethos is grounded in a social regard for one's foes, recognizing their abilities and the common quest for greatness.

Abdulmanap's way to deal with deference is apparent in the lead of his warriors, quite epitomized by Khabib Nurmagomedov. Khabib's post-battle activities, like aiding fallen adversaries or showing sportsmanship in triumph, mirror the qualities imparted by his mentor.

Abdulmanap's impact goes past specialized preparing; it includes a set of rules that underlines the human parts of contest, encouraging a climate where regard is as essential to progress as any actual expertise.

The solidarity cultivated in Abdulmanap's rec center rises above the singular quests for contenders, making a feeling of brotherhood and common perspective. Dagestan, set apart by its assorted nationalities and etymological varieties, faces authentic difficulties connected with character and regionalism. Abdulmanap's instructing reasoning turns into a scaffold that unites contenders from various foundations under a typical standard of Dagestani pride. The solidarity fashioned in the rec center turns into a microcosm of the more extensive cultural solidarity that Abdulmanap imagines for Dagestan.

This feeling of solidarity isn't restricted to the exercise center; it reaches out to the worldwide phase of MMA. Contenders prepared by Abdulmanap, including Khabib Nurmagomedov, became diplomats for Dagestan as well as for a common social personality. The solidarity encouraged in Abdulmanap's rec center fills in as a demonstration of the possibility that, in spite of verifiable intricacies and outer discernments, Dagestanis can join under a shared objective, epitomizing a strength that emerges from variety.

The acknowledgment of Abdulmanap's endeavors in advancing discipline, regard, and solidarity stretches out past the prompt domain of MMA. His instructing reasoning has gathered reverence and regard from the worldwide MMA people group, procuring him acknowledgment as a coach and directing figure. Individual mentors, contenders, and fans recognize the special mix of social qualities and specialized aptitude that separates Abdulmanap in the frequently extreme and cutthroat universe of blended hand to hand fighting.

The discipline imparted by Abdulmanap is tangible in the careful preparation regimens and vital methodologies utilized by his warriors. The regard they display, for their rivals as well as for the actual game, turns into a distinctive component. The solidarity encouraged in the exercise center makes a cooperative soul that goes past individual accomplishments, adding to a more extensive story of social pride and flexibility.

The acknowledgment of Abdulmanap's effect is especially clear in the outcome of Khabib Nurmagomedov's retirement. The worldwide flood of regard and appreciation from contenders, mentors, and fans the same featured the significant impact Abdulmanap had on his child's vocation and character. Accolades poured in, not only for the specialized ability bestowed by Abdulmanap however for the upsides of discipline, regard, and solidarity that characterized Khabib's excursion.

Discipline, with regards to Abdulmanap's training, stretches out to the improvement of a contender's personality. The difficulties looked inside the octagon are much of the time reflected by life's preliminaries beyond it.

Abdulmanap's accentuation on discipline turns into a core value for exploring the two fields. The psychological strength created through focused preparing converts into flexibility notwithstanding misfortune, repeating the more extensive topic of Dagestani determination.

Regard, as supported by Abdulmanap, is certainly not a one-layered idea. It includes a profound comprehension of one's rivals, perceiving their assets and weaknesses. This nuanced way to deal with deference stretches out past the game, molding the manner in which contenders draw in with the world. The modesty imparted by Abdulmanap turns into an establishment for individual and expert achievement, making competitors who are gifted as well as grounded in their way to deal with life.

Solidarity, as a fundamental belief in Abdulmanap's training reasoning, has more extensive ramifications for cultural union. Dagestan, with its assorted ethnic gatherings and dialects, faces interesting difficulties connected with regionalism and character. Abdulmanap's exercise center turns into a microcosm of a unified Dagestani front, representing that in spite of contrasts, a common social legacy can be a bringing together power. This solidarity stretches out to the worldwide stage, where warriors from Dagestan become diplomats for an aggregate character that goes past individual accomplishments.

The effect of Abdulmanap's training reasoning on discipline, regard, and solidarity is likewise obvious in the mentorship he gave striving for mentors. His direction reached out past the specialized parts of preparing, enveloping the complexities of imparting values in the up and coming age of warriors. Abdulmanap's job as a coach mirrors the profundity of his obligation to create fruitful warriors as well as to add to the more extensive improvement of the MMA people group.

The tradition of discipline, regard, and solidarity advanced by Abdulmanap is a living demonstration of the getting through effect of a that the mentor values imparted in the exercise center resound a long ways past the octagon. The acknowledgment of his endeavors reaches out past the honors and titles won by his warriors; it envelops a social and philosophical commitment to the universe of blended hand to hand fighting. Abdulmanap's heritage turns into a wellspring of motivation for warriors, mentors, and fans around the world, featuring that outcome in sports isn't just about triumphs yet about the person and values that characterize a competitor's excursion.

Abdulmanap Nurmagomedov's backing for discipline, regard, and solidarity goes past the limits of a mentor's job; it turns into a groundbreaking power that shapes the personality of people and the ethos of the more extensive blended combative techniques (MMA) people group. His inheritance is a demonstration of the getting through force of values that reach out past the quick quest for triumph and titles.

Discipline, as imparted by Abdulmanap, is definitely not an unbending inconvenience of rules yet a comprehensive way to deal with individual and expert turn of events. It includes the development of a restrained mentality that saturates each part of a warrior's life. The restrained way to deal with preparing, nourishment, and mental determination turns into a layout for exploring the intricacies of the game and life past it. Abdulmanap's training reasoning perceives that discipline isn't just a necessary evil yet a deep rooted quality that cultivates strength notwithstanding challenges.

The discipline learned in Abdulmanap's rec center is described by consistency, devotion, and a pledge to persistent improvement. Warriors under his direction foster a hard working attitude that stretches out past the spotlight of the octagon, impacting their decisions, propensities, and way to deal with difficulty. Abdulmanap's accentuation on discipline turns into an establishment for individual and expert achievement, making competitors who are truly gifted as well as have the psychological backbone to endure despite misfortunes.

Regard, in Abdulmanap's training reasoning, is certainly not a latent affirmation yet a functioning commitment with one's rivals, the game, and its customs. The regard ingrained by Abdulmanap includes a comprehension of the penances and difficulties looked by each warrior. It rises above the serious field, molding the manner in which contenders act in triumph and rout. The modesty displayed by Abdulmanap's warriors turns into an impression of the regard imbued in their personality.

Abdulmanap's warriors, especially exemplified by Khabib Nurmagomedov, grandstand a regard that stretches out past the limits of the game. Khabib's connections with rivals, authorities, and the more extensive MMA people group mirror a profound comprehension of the interconnectedness of the contenders and the common excursion they embrace. Abdulmanap's impact isn't simply in the specialized abilities granted however in the making of contenders who approach their vocations with a significant feeling of sportsmanship.

Solidarity, a fundamental belief in Abdulmanap's training, turns into a limiting power that goes past the singular quests for warriors. The rec center under his direction turns into a local area where variety is embraced, and an aggregate feeling of direction is developed. The solidarity fashioned in the exercise center isn't restricted to instructional meetings; it stretches out to the manner in which warriors support one another, celebrate triumphs, and explore routs. Abdulmanap's vision of solidarity turns into a microcosm of the cultural union he imagines for Dagestan and then some.

The acknowledgment of Abdulmanap's endeavors in advancing discipline, regard, and solidarity is clear in the effect on the MMA people group at large. Individual mentors, contenders, and fans recognize the unmistakable social and philosophical commitments that put Abdulmanap aside.

His inheritance turns into a reference point for those looking for specialized greatness as well as a more profound comprehension of the qualities that characterize a military craftsman's excursion.

Abdulmanap's impact on discipline, regard, and solidarity is a heritage that reaches out to the up and coming age of contenders and mentors. Hopeful competitors who enter his exercise center are not just prepared in the specialized parts of the game yet are submerged in a culture that values character improvement, common regard, and aggregate development. The acknowledgment of this approach draws in people looking for more than athletic achievement — it draws the people who comprehend that genuine significance is estimated by triumphs as well as by the positive effect one has on the existences of others.

The tradition of Abdulmanap's training reasoning isn't bound to the honors and titles won by his contenders. It lives on in the accounts of discipline, regard, and solidarity that keep on molding the stories of MMA. The effect is obvious in the more extensive discussions about sportsmanship, the job of mentors, and the social subtleties that impact the MMA scene. Abdulmanap's heritage turns into a wellspring of motivation for the people who comprehend that genuine progress in sports includes more than actual ability — it includes the development of character and the epitome of values that rise above the prompt domain of contest.

The acknowledgment of Abdulmanap Nurmagomedov's endeavors in advancing discipline, regard, and solidarity is a demonstration of the getting through impact of a mentor whose heritage arrives at past the octagon. The qualities imparted by Abdulmanap rise above the quick quest for triumphs, becoming core values for a daily routine very much experienced. As the MMA people group considers his commitments, Abdulmanap's heritage fills in as an update that genuine significance in sports isn't just estimated by titles however by the positive effect a mentor can have on the person and ethos of those under his direction.

5.3 Testimonials from community members and leaders on his positive impact.

Abdulmanap Nurmagomedov's positive effect reached out a long ways past the limits of the exercise center, resounding profoundly inside the local area of Dagestan and then some. Tributes from local area individuals and pioneers give strong bits of knowledge into the significant and enduring impact he had on the existences of people, the advancement of Dagestan, and the more extensive social scene.

In Dagestan, a locale set apart by its rich social embroidery and verifiable intricacies, Abdulmanap Nurmagomedov arose as a groundbreaking figure whose effect arrived at each side of the local area. Tributes from neighborhood inhabitants portray a mentor whose impact went past the domain of sports, contacting the hearts and psyches of the people who saw his commitment to local area improvement.

Local area individuals frequently talk about Abdulmanap's obligation to giving open doors to the adolescent. From arranging wrestling competitions in far off towns to laying out preparing offices in less favored regions, his endeavors were aimed at enabling the future. Tributes frequently feature the substantial distinction these drives made in the existences of youthful people, offering them a pathway to emphatically channel their energies.

Pioneers in the Dagestani people group recognize Abdulmanap's job as an impetus for positive change. Tributes from nearby authorities and local area pioneers highlight the effect of his drives in tending to financial variations. By making spaces for athletic improvement in districts with restricted assets, Abdulmanap turned into an image of strength and strengthening. His heritage, as communicated in these tributes, is inseparable from the possibility that local area improvement isn't simply a dream yet a substantial obligation to making a superior future for Dagestan.

Instructive drives advocated by Abdulmanap likewise earned far and wide acknowledgment from local area individuals and pioneers the same. Tributes frequently feature the grants gave to promising understudies, underlining the extraordinary force of schooling in forming the eventual fate of Dagestan. Abdulmanap's impact, as reverberated in these tributes, isn't restricted to the rec center; it reaches out to supporting an age with scholarly ability and a promise to local area administration.

The protection of conventional Dagestani hand to hand fighting is a subject that reverberates in tributes from social pioneers and devotees. Abdulmanap's part in guaranteeing that conventional tackling methods are passed down to people in the future is many times celebrated as an essential component of social safeguarding. Tributes feature his endeavors to make preparing focuses that attention on athletic advancement as well as act as watchmen of social legacy.

Social pioneers offer thanks for Abdulmanap's commitments to the more extensive Dagestani personality. Tributes frequently underline that his work goes past delivering fruitful contenders; it includes making envoys for Dagestani culture on the worldwide stage. The outcome of contenders prepared under Abdulmanap turns into a wellspring of aggregate pride, supporting the rich embroidery of Dagestani customs.

The tributes from neighborhood occupants likewise address Abdulmanap's job as a coach and mentor. Past the rec center, he turned into a wellspring of motivation and direction for some people, especially the young. Tributes frequently feature the effect of his useful tidbits, the accentuation on discipline, and the instillation of values that reach out a long ways past the quick domain of sports.

The sad loss of Abdulmanap in 2020 evoked a flood of tributes that mirrored the profundity of his effect on the local area. Occupants, pioneers, and social figures joined in communicating misery, appreciation, and a common acknowledgment of the void left by his flight. These tributes turned into an aggregate articulation of grieving, mirroring the significant association Abdulmanap had with individuals of Dagestan.

Past Dagestan, the tributes from public and worldwide figures highlight the worldwide reach of Abdulmanap's positive effect. Pioneers in the realm of MMA, individual mentors, and warriors from around the globe have shared their appearance on the tradition of Abdulmanap Nurmagomedov. Tributes frequently center around the remarkable mix of social qualities, training ability, and individual moxy that put him aside in the serious scene of blended hand to hand fighting.

Individual mentors address the extraordinary impact Abdulmanap had on the training calling. Tributes frequently feature his capacity to offset customary instructing strategies with imaginative methodologies, making a training reasoning that rises above social and geological limits. The effect on the MMA training local area is recognized as a demonstration of Abdulmanap's one of a kind vision and obligation to greatness.

Warriors who prepared under Abdulmanap offer the absolute most piercing tributes, pondering the significant job he played in their professions and self-awareness. Tributes frequently underline the protective direction, the steadfast help, and the priceless life examples bestowed by Abdulmanap. The connection among mentor and warrior, as communicated in these tributes, goes past the specialized parts of preparing; it includes a profound and getting through association that formed their way of living.

Worldwide figures inside the MMA people group honor Abdulmanap's job in lifting Dagestani combative techniques on the worldwide stage. Tributes frequently feature the effect of contenders like Khabib Nurmagomedov as social envoys who carried a one of a kind arrangement of values to the universe of MMA. Abdulmanap's heritage, as found in these tributes, reaches out to reshaping discernments and encouraging a more extensive appreciation for the rich practices of Dagestan.

The tributes from local area individuals, pioneers, and figures inside the MMA people group on the whole paint a picture of Abdulmanap

Nurmagomedov as a figure whose positive effect rises above limits. His inheritance is one of strengthening, social pride, and mentorship that arrives at past the exercise center and the prompt domain of sports. Tributes become a chorale of voices, each communicating a special feature of the significant impact Abdulmanap had on people, networks, and the worldwide scene of blended hand to hand fighting.

Abdulmanap Nurmagomedov's positive effect, as reverberated in tributes, is a demonstration of the getting through tradition of a the mentor limits of sports, turning into a signal of motivation and strengthening for people and networks the same.

Inside Dagestan, tributes from local area individuals mirror a profound feeling of appreciation for Abdulmanap's obligation to giving open doors to the young. His drives, for example, putting together wrestling competitions in far off towns, are many times depicted as groundbreaking minutes that opened entryways for youthful gifts. Tributes convey the substantial effect of these endeavors, portraying a mentor who had faith in the capability of each and every person, no matter what their experience or conditions.

Pioneers in the Dagestani people group underscore Abdulmanap's job as an impetus for positive change. Tributes from neighborhood authorities and local area pioneers feature the financial effect of his drives, especially in districts confronting difficulties of restricted assets. Abdulmanap's heritage, as communicated in these tributes, becomes inseparable from versatility and strengthening, exhibiting the extraordinary force of sports in tending to more extensive cultural variations.

Instructive drives supported by Abdulmanap get honors in tributes that highlight the extraordinary force of training in forming Dagestan's future. Grants for promising understudies are praised as a demonstration of Abdulmanap's obligation to comprehensive turn of events. Tributes frequently express how these instructive drives, under his direction, became pathways for people to break liberated from restrictions and seek after a more promising time to come.

Social pioneers and lovers in Dagestan offer tributes that feature Abdulmanap's job in saving customary combative techniques. The foundation of preparing focuses that emphasis on athletic ability as well as on the protecting of social legacy is recognized as a vital commitment. Tributes frequently offer thanks for a the mentor significance of crossing over the past and the present, guaranteeing that Dagestan's rich customs keep on flourishing.

The more extensive effect on the Dagestani character is underscored in tributes from social pioneers. Abdulmanap's part in making diplomats for Dagestani culture on the worldwide stage is praised as a wellspring of aggregate pride. The progress of contenders prepared under his direction turns into a social story that reverberates a long ways past the boundaries of Dagestan, molding discernments and cultivating a feeling of solidarity and character.

Tributes from nearby inhabitants likewise convey the profoundly private effect of Abdulmanap's mentorship. Past the exercise center, he arises as a mentor and a wellspring of motivation for some. The tributes frequently feature the extraordinary impact of his useful tidbits, the accentuation on discipline, and the instillation of values that go past the domain of sports. Abdulmanap turns into a directing light for the young, imparting in them a feeling of direction and heading.

The worldwide tributes from figures inside the MMA people group highlight Abdulmanap's worldwide reach and impact. Individual mentors recognize the extraordinary effect he had on the training calling, mixing conventional techniques with creative methodologies. Tributes frequently express how Abdulmanap's one of a kind training reasoning reverberated with mentors around the world, making a gradually expanding influence that rises above social and topographical limits.

Warriors prepared under Abdulmanap offer tributes that dig into the significant connection among mentor and competitor. The effect of his caring direction, steadfast help, and life illustrations are clearly expressed. Tributes offer the profundity of thanks and regard contenders feel, for the specialized abilities bestowed, yet for the mentorship that molded their personality and affected their way of living.

Worldwide figures inside the MMA people group honor Abdulmanap's part in lifting Dagestani hand to hand fighting on the worldwide stage. Tributes frequently feature the more extensive effect of contenders like Khabib Nurmagomedov as social ministers, reshaping insights and encouraging a more profound appreciation for the social lavishness of Dagestan. Abdulmanap's heritage, as found in these tributes, turns into a scaffold that interfaces societies and grandstands the widespread qualities implanted in the realm of blended hand to hand fighting.

The tributes from local area individuals, pioneers, and figures inside the MMA people group all in all paint a mosaic of Abdulmanap Nurmagomedov's positive effect. His heritage is an orchestra of appreciation, strengthening, and social pride that resounds across ages and rises above topographical limits. The tributes become a chorale of voices, each adding to the story of a mentor whose impact went a long ways past the triumphs in the octagon, making a permanent imprint on the existences of people and the social scene of Dagestan and the world.

8

Chapter 6

Abdulmanap's Philosophies

Abdulmanap Nurmagomedov's training theory is an embroidery woven with social subtleties, conventional qualities, and a remarkable mix of intelligence gained through private encounters. His way to deal with training, coaching, and combative techniques guidance mirrors a comprehensive vision that reaches out past the bounds of the rec center, enveloping life examples, social safeguarding, and the improvement of balanced people. As we dive into Abdulmanap's methods of reasoning, we unwind the layers of shrewdness that extraordinarily affect the universe of blended combative techniques (MMA).

At the center of Abdulmanap's instructing reasoning is the accentuation on discipline as a central mainstay of progress. Conceived out of his own encounters in Dagestan, where monetary difficulties and cultural assumptions could without much of a stretch become sidetracked, discipline turned into a core value for Abdulmanap. His instructing goes past the simple adherence to preparing plans and actual schedules; it stretches out to the development of mental backbone and profound flexibility. Discipline, in Abdulmanap's way of thinking, is an all encompassing methodology that shapes the competitor's presentation inside the octagon as well as their personality beyond it.

Abdulmanap's instructing reasoning in regards to teach is well established in the thorough preparation customs of Dagestani wrestling. These customs, went down through ages, structure the establishment whereupon he constructs the psychological and actual strength of his contenders. The examples learned in the exercise center become a microcosm of life's difficulties, getting ready warriors for triumph inside the octagon as well as for the more extensive excursion of individual and expert development.

Regard is one more foundation of Abdulmanap's training reasoning, intelligent of the social ethos of Dagestan. In a game frequently portrayed by extreme competitions and pre-battle showy behaviors, Abdulmanap's accentuation on regard turns into a distinctive component. This regard reaches out to adversaries, mentors, authorities, and the actual game. Abdulmanap's training reasoning includes ingraining a profound comprehension of one's foes, perceiving their abilities, and recognizing the common quest for greatness. The modesty imparted by Abdulmanap turns into an establishment for individual and expert achievement, making competitors who are talented as well as grounded in their way to deal with life.

Solidarity, as a basic belief in Abdulmanap's training reasoning, goes past the singular quests for warriors. His exercise center turns into a local area where variety is embraced, and an aggregate feeling of direction is developed. Dagestan, set apart by its assorted nationalities and etymological varieties, faces authentic difficulties connected with character and regionalism. Abdulmanap's instructing reasoning turns into a scaffold that unites warriors from various foundations under a typical standard of Dagestani pride. The solidarity manufactured in the rec center turns into a microcosm of the more extensive cultural solidarity that Abdulmanap imagines for Dagestan.

The interconnectedness of discipline, regard, and solidarity in Abdulmanap's training reasoning makes a comprehensive system for the improvement of warriors. The illustrations advanced inside the rec center become life rules that stretch out past the domain of sports. This all encompassing methodology is intelligent of Abdulmanap's profound comprehension that the quintessence of a military craftsman goes past the limits of the octagon — it includes the development of character, flexibility, and a pledge to values that endure everyday hardship.

Social conservation is a vital feature of Abdulmanap's training theory, appearing in his dynamic advancement of customary Dagestani wrestling strategies. This obligation to saving the unmistakable military fine arts went down through ages guarantees that the rich social legacy of Dagestan stays lively and pertinent. Abdulmanap's instructing reasoning includes coordinating these conventional procedures with current games science, showing a nuanced way to deal with social safeguarding. It's an acknowledgment that custom can be a wellspring of solidarity, giving an establishment to flexibility and character, even notwithstanding developing cultural elements.

Abdulmanap's instructing reasoning additionally includes the fragile harmony among custom and advancement. Dagestan, in the same way as other districts with a rich social history, faces the test of exploring social protection in the midst of the powers of globalization and cultural change. His methodology, which embraces custom while consolidating present day preparing systems, turns into a model for exploring this perplexing landscape. Abdulmanap's training reasoning mirrors a powerful comprehension that custom can be a wellspring of solidarity, giving an establishment to versatility and personality even notwithstanding developing cultural elements.

Abdulmanap's training reasoning is profoundly interwoven with his vision for the more extensive Dagestani people group. His drives in giving open doors to the young, sorting out wrestling competitions in nearby networks, and laying out preparing focuses are not just about making fruitful contenders; they are about strengthening and local area improvement. The grassroots way to deal with sports, supported by Abdulmanap, is a demonstration of his conviction that sports can be a groundbreaking power, offering a pathway for youthful gifts to helpfully channel their energies.

In Abdulmanap's training theory, schooling isn't discrete from athletic preparation; it is a cooperative relationship that he underscores. Grants for promising understudies, consolation for contenders to seek after schooling close by sports, and an all encompassing way to deal with improvement highlight his obligation to sustaining balanced people. Abdulmanap's instructing reasoning becomes interwoven with the instructive yearnings of Dagestani youth, offering them a pathway to progress that envelops both scholarly and actual greatness.

The tributes from local area individuals and pioneers offer a brief look into this present reality effect of Abdulmanap's training reasoning. His accentuation on discipline, regard, solidarity, and social safeguarding has made a heritage that reaches out a long ways past the rec center. It's a tradition of strengthening, local area improvement, and social pride — a demonstration of the extraordinary force of sports when directed by a way of thinking that goes past triumphs and titles.

Abdulmanap's instructing reasoning turns into a living illustration of how sports can be a vehicle for positive change, imparting values that shape people and networks. His vision for the adolescent, his obligation to saving social customs, and his faith in the groundbreaking force of schooling are not simply hypothetical standards — they are typified in the tales of people whose lives were moved by his training reasoning.

Abdulmanap Nurmagomedov's instructing reasoning is a comprehensive vision that rises above the limits of the octagon. His accentuation on discipline, regard, solidarity, social conservation, and local area improvement mirrors a significant comprehension of the groundbreaking force of sports.

Abdulmanap's instructing reasoning turns into a directing light for competitors, mentors, and networks, offering a diagram for progress that goes past the prompt quest for triumphs and titles. A way of thinking leaves a getting through inheritance — a heritage that proceeds to rouse and deeply mold the existences of those contacted by the extraordinary insight of a mentor whose effect arrives at a long ways past the universe of blended hand to hand fighting.

6.1 Exploration of Abdulmanap's philosophical approach to martial arts and life.

Abdulmanap Nurmagomedov's philosophical way to deal with combative techniques and life is a rich embroidery woven with social bits of knowledge, individual encounters, and a novel mix of shrewdness that rises above the limits of the rec center. As we investigate his significant way of thinking, we dive into the layers of believed that have molded his training strategies, his viewpoint on life, and the getting through influence he has left on the universe of blended combative techniques (MMA).

Integral to Abdulmanap's philosophical methodology is the possibility that hand to hand fighting isn't simply an actual undertaking yet a comprehensive excursion including mental, profound, and otherworldly aspects. Drawing from his Dagestani roots, where combative techniques are profoundly imbued in the social texture, Abdulmanap considers the training to be a way to self-revelation and self-improvement. For his purposes, the exercise center turns into a dojo of life, where contenders level up their actual abilities as well as develop discipline, flexibility, and a more profound comprehension of themselves.

Discipline remains as a foundation in Abdulmanap's philosophical structure. Established in the conventional wrestling customs of Dagestan, where thorough preparation is a lifestyle, discipline isn't only a bunch of rules yet a core value that shapes the personality of his warriors. Abdulmanap's way of thinking on discipline stretches out past the limits of preparing plans and actual schedules; it includes the improvement of mental grit, unfaltering responsibility, and a feeling of obligation that goes past the quick requests of the game.

The way of thinking of discipline, as granted by Abdulmanap, is an acknowledgment that the difficulties looked inside the rec center mirror the difficulties experienced throughout everyday life. The psychological flexibility created through focused preparing turns into an important resource in exploring the intricacies of the world. Abdulmanap's training reasoning considers discipline to be a device for self-awareness, imparting in warriors the solidarity to persist despite rivals as well as even with life's difficulties.

Regard is one more central component in Abdulmanap's philosophical methodology. Conceived out of the social ethos of Dagestan, where regard for one's foes is profoundly imbued, Abdulmanap's training reasoning includes imparting a significant comprehension of the mankind in contest.

Regard, in his view, is diverse — it stretches out to rivals, mentors, authorities, and the actual game. It's anything but a shallow politeness yet a profound affirmation of the common quest for greatness.

Abdulmanap's way of thinking on regard becomes apparent in the lead of his contenders, generally outstandingly encapsulated by Khabib Nurmagomedov. Khabib's post-battle activities, like aiding fallen rivals or showing sportsmanship in triumph, mirror the qualities imparted by his mentor. Abdulmanap's instructing reasoning includes going past the specialized parts of the game; it incorporates an overarching set of principles that underscores the human parts of contest. Warriors under his direction figure out how to explore the serious contentions of MMA with a regard that rises above the cutthroat field.

Solidarity shapes one more fundamental part of Abdulmanap's philosophical methodology. In a locale like Dagestan, set apart by different identities and etymological varieties, Abdulmanap's training theory turns into a bringing together power. The rec center under his direction turns into a microcosm of a unified Dagestani front, representing that in spite of verifiable intricacies and outer discernments, Dagestanis can join under a shared objective. The solidarity encouraged in the rec center turns into a microcosm of the more extensive cultural solidarity that Abdulmanap imagines for his country.

The way of thinking of solidarity reaches out to the worldwide phase of MMA. Contenders prepared by Abdulmanap, including Khabib Nurmagomedov, become diplomats for Dagestan as well as for a common social character. The solidarity encouraged in Abdulmanap's exercise center fills in as a demonstration of the possibility that, notwithstanding verifiable intricacies and outside discernments, Dagestanis can join under a shared objective. This solidarity stretches out to the worldwide stage, where contenders from Dagestan become diplomats for an aggregate personality that goes past individual accomplishments.

Social conservation is a philosophical topic profoundly implanted in Abdulmanap's methodology. Dagestan, with its rich history and unmistakable social practices, faces the test of protecting its legacy in a quickly impacting world. Abdulmanap's way of thinking includes protecting as well as effectively advancing customary Dagestani wrestling procedures. The foundation of preparing fixates that emphasis on both athletic turn of events and the defending of social legacy is a demonstration of his obligation to social conservation.

Abdulmanap's training reasoning perceives that custom can be a wellspring of solidarity, giving an establishment to versatility and character even despite developing cultural elements. The combination of conventional combative techniques with current preparation philosophies features a nuanced way to deal with social conservation. Abdulmanap's way of thinking turns into an extension that interfaces the past and the present, guaranteeing that the rich embroidery of Dagestani customs keeps on thriving.

The interconnectedness of Abdulmanap's philosophical topics makes an extensive system for hand to hand fighting and life. His methodology goes past the details of preparing; it turns into a comprehensive way of thinking that shapes the person, values, and perspective of his contenders. The exercise center, under his direction, changes into a dojo where contenders level up their actual abilities as well as go through an extraordinary excursion of self-revelation.

Abdulmanap's philosophical way to deal with combative techniques and life is likewise thought about in his perspectives schooling. For his purposes, schooling isn't discrete from athletic preparation; an interlaced excursion cultivates balanced people. The grants gave to promising understudies, the support for contenders to seek after training close by sports, and the comprehensive way to deal with improvement highlight his obligation to sustaining people who succeed both mentally and actually.

The investigation of Abdulmanap's philosophical methodology uncovers a mentor whose vision stretches out a long ways past the prompt domain of blended hand to hand fighting. His training reasoning turns into a core value for competitors looking for triumphs in the octagon as well as a more profound comprehension of themselves and their spot on the planet. Abdulmanap's lessons are not restricted to the rec center; they are life illustrations that reverberate with the intricacies of presence.

Abdulmanap Nurmagomedov's philosophical way to deal with hand to hand fighting and life encapsulates a significant comprehension of the interconnectedness between actual preparation and self-improvement. As we dig further into his way of thinking, we unwind extra layers of intelligence that enduringly affect the universe of blended hand to hand fighting (MMA) and the existences of those he has contacted.

Fundamental to Abdulmanap's philosophical methodology is the conviction that combative techniques fills in as a vehicle for self-disclosure and self-awareness. His training techniques reach out past the details of battling; they embrace the possibility that the difficulties looked inside the rec center mirror the difficulties experienced throughout everyday life. This comprehensive viewpoint positions the rec center as a microcosm of life's intricacies, where contenders refine their actual abilities as well as develop mental flexibility, the capacity to appreciate individuals on a profound level, and a more profound comprehension of themselves.

Discipline, an essential component in Abdulmanap's way of thinking, isn't just a bunch of rules or an unbending construction forced on his warriors. A unique power pervades each part of the warrior's excursion. Abdulmanap's way of thinking on discipline is a call to foster a restrained outlook that reaches out past preparation plans and actual schedules. This mentality turns into a core value for exploring life's vulnerabilities, helping warriors to move toward difficulties with faithful responsibility, consistency, and a feeling of obligation.

Regard, one more foundation of Abdulmanap's way of thinking, is well established in the social ethos of Dagestan. His training reaches out past the specialized parts of battling to impart a significant comprehension of humankind in rivalry. Regard turns into a multi-layered idea, enveloping rivals, mentors, authorities, and the actual game. Abdulmanap's training reasoning includes developing a profound affirmation of the common quest for greatness, encouraging a feeling of sportsmanship that rises above the cutthroat field.

The philosophical subject of solidarity in Abdulmanap's methodology stretches out to the worldwide phase of MMA. Warriors prepared under his direction become delegates of Dagestan as well as diplomats for a common social character. The solidarity encouraged in Abdulmanap's exercise center fills in as a demonstration of the possibility that, notwithstanding verifiable intricacies and outside discernments, Dagestanis can join under a shared objective. This solidarity reaches out to the worldwide stage, where warriors from Dagestan become representatives for an aggregate character that goes past individual accomplishments.

Social protection stays a powerful topic in Abdulmanap's philosophical methodology. Dagestan, a district with a rich history and unmistakable social practices, faces the test of protecting its legacy in a quickly impacting world. Abdulmanap's instructing reasoning includes protecting as well as effectively advancing customary Dagestani wrestling methods. The foundation of preparing fixates that emphasis on both athletic turn of events and the defending of social legacy is a demonstration of his obligation to social protection.

Abdulmanap's way of thinking perceives that custom can be a wellspring of solidarity, giving an establishment to flexibility and personality even notwithstanding developing cultural elements. The joining of customary combative techniques with present day preparing procedures grandstands a nuanced way to deal with social protection.

Abdulmanap's way of thinking turns into a scaffold that interfaces the past and the present, guaranteeing that the rich embroidery of Dagestani customs keeps on prospering.

Abdulmanap's philosophical way to deal with hand to hand fighting and life likewise underscores the worth of schooling as a vital piece of self-improvement. His vision sees schooling not as a different substance from athletic preparation but rather as an interlaced excursion that encourages balanced people. The grants gave to promising understudies, the support for warriors to seek after instruction close by sports, and the all encompassing way to deal with improvement highlight his obligation to sustaining people who succeed both mentally and actually.

The investigation of Abdulmanap's philosophical methodology uncovers a mentor whose vision reaches out a long ways past the quick domain of blended combative techniques. His training reasoning turns into a core value for competitors looking for triumphs in the octagon as well as a more profound comprehension of themselves and their spot on the planet.

Abdulmanap's lessons are not restricted to the rec center; they are life illustrations that resound with the intricacies of presence.

In taking into account Abdulmanap's way of thinking, it's fundamental to perceive the more extensive effect of his lessons on the MMA people group and then some. His inheritance isn't exclusively characterized by the triumphs of his warriors yet by the persevering through rules that shape the person and perspective of those he tutored.

The interconnectedness of discipline, regard, solidarity, social conservation, and schooling in Abdulmanap's way of thinking makes a complete structure for hand to hand fighting and life. His methodology goes past the details of preparing; it turns into an all encompassing way of thinking that shapes the person, values, and perspective of his contenders. The rec center, under his direction, changes into a dojo where warriors level up their actual abilities as well as go through an extraordinary excursion of self-disclosure.

In taking into account Abdulmanap's way of thinking, it's fundamental to perceive the more extensive effect of his lessons on the MMA people group and then some. His inheritance isn't exclusively characterized by the triumphs of his contenders however by the getting through rules that shape the person and perspective of those he coached.

Abdulmanap Nurmagomedov s philosophical way to deal with hand to hand fighting and life is a significant embroidery woven with strings of discipline, regard, solidarity, social conservation, and schooling. His instructing reasoning goes past the details of the game; it turns into a core value for an extraordinary excursion that reaches out past the bounds of the rec center. Abdulmanap's effect isn't just in that frame of mind of his warriors however in the getting through tradition of people who encapsulate the standards of his philosophical methodology, molding the universe of blended hand to hand fighting as well as the more extensive scene of life itself.

6.2 Examination of key principles and values that shaped his coaching style.

Abdulmanap Nurmagomedov's training style is well established in a bunch of key standards and values that reflect his Dagestani legacy as well as a significant comprehension of combative techniques as an extraordinary excursion. As we inspect the groundworks of his training, we disentangle the standards and values that have formed his particular methodology and made a permanent imprint on the universe of blended hand to hand fighting (MMA).

1. **Discipline:**

   Abdulmanap Nurmagomedov's training style is inseparable from discipline. This essential standard is profoundly imbued in the customary wrestling customs of Dagestan, where thorough preparation isn't simply a routine however a lifestyle.

   Discipline, in Abdulmanap's instructing reasoning, isn't restricted to the actual parts of preparing; it stretches out to the improvement of mental guts, close to home flexibility, and a feeling of obligation. Warriors under his direction discover that discipline isn't just about complying with preparing plans; a mentality shapes character and sets them up for the difficulties inside and outside the octagon.

This accentuation on discipline mirrors Abdulmanap's conviction that the illustrations learned in the rec center mirror the difficulties experienced throughout everyday life. The psychological versatility created through focused preparing turns into a significant resource in exploring the intricacies of the world. Contenders, under Abdulmanap's training, typify a restrained methodology that reaches out past the quick requests of the game and turns into a directing power for individual and expert achievement.

2. **Regard:**

Regard remains as a foundation in Abdulmanap's training style. Established in the social ethos of Dagestan, where regard for one's enemies is profoundly imbued, Abdulmanap imparts in his warriors a significant comprehension of mankind in rivalry. Regard, in his training reasoning, goes past shallow cordialities; it includes a profound affirmation of the common quest for greatness. Contenders figure out how to move toward rivals, mentors, authorities, and the actual game with a feeling of regard that rises above the serious field.

This standard of regard is clear in the lead of his warriors, both inside and outside the octagon. Khabib Nurmagomedov, perhaps of Abdulmanap's most eminent understudy, embodies this worth through activities like aiding fallen adversaries and showing sportsmanship in triumph. Abdulmanap's instructing style includes imparting an overarching set of principles that stresses the human parts of rivalry, cultivating a feeling of regard that turns into an essential piece of his warriors' personalities.

3. **Solidarity:**

Abdulmanap's training style is portrayed by the way of thinking of solidarity. In a locale like Dagestan, set apart by different identities and semantic varieties, his exercise center turns into a microcosm of a unified Dagestani front. This solidarity mirrors Abdulmanap's vision of cultural solidarity, rising above authentic intricacies and outside discernments. The rec center, under his direction, turns into a space where warriors from various foundations join under a shared objective, exhibiting the force of aggregate exertion.

The way of thinking of solidarity reaches out to the worldwide phase of MMA. Contenders prepared by Abdulmanap, including Khabib Nurmagomedov, become delegates of Dagestan as well as ministers for a common social personality. The solidarity encouraged in Abdulmanap's rec center fills in as a demonstration of the possibility that, notwithstanding verifiable intricacies and outer discernments, Dagestanis can join under a shared objective.

This solidarity reaches out to the worldwide stage, where warriors from Dagestan become diplomats for an aggregate character that goes past individual accomplishments.

4. **Social Protection:**

Social protection is a central part of Abdulmanap's training style. Dagestan, with its rich history and unmistakable social practices, faces the test of protecting its legacy in a quickly impacting world. Abdulmanap's training reasoning includes protecting as well as effectively advancing conventional Dagestani wrestling strategies. The foundation of preparing fixates that emphasis on both athletic turn of events and the shielding of social legacy is a demonstration of his obligation to social conservation.

His instructing style mirrors a nuanced approach that incorporates customary combative techniques with current preparation procedures. This coordination exhibits Abdulmanap's comprehension that custom can be a wellspring of solidarity, giving an establishment to strength and personality even despite developing cultural elements. The safeguarding of social legacy turns into an essential piece of his instructing style, guaranteeing that the rich embroidered artwork of Dagestani customs keeps on prospering.

5. **Comprehensive Turn of events:**

Abdulmanap's training style is revolved around the possibility of all encompassing turn of events. For his purposes, hand to hand fighting isn't just about actual ability; a groundbreaking excursion envelops mental, close to home, and profound aspects. His training goes past the specialized parts of battling to develop balanced people. Discipline, regard, solidarity, and social conservation are not disengaged standards but rather interconnected components in the all encompassing improvement of his contenders.

Instruction is a significant part of Abdulmanap's training style, entwined with athletic preparation to encourage people who succeed both mentally and truly. The grants gave to promising understudies and the consolation for contenders to seek after training close by sports highlight his obligation to supporting people who are gifted warriors as well as knowledgeable supporters of society.

6. **Paternal Direction:**

A particular component of Abdulmanap's training style is his job as a mentor. Past the specialized parts of preparing, he gives mentorship and direction that stretch out to life outside the exercise center. Warriors frequently talk about the significant effect of his useful tidbits, underscoring the significance of discipline, regard, and values that go past the domain of sports. Abdulmanap's instructing style includes forming warriors' athletic capacities as well as sustaining their personality and giving a strong, caring presence.

This caring direction turns into a wellspring of motivation for some contenders, especially the young. Abdulmanap's training style includes imparting not just the abilities required for outcome in the octagon yet additionally life examples that shape the direction of his warriors' lives. The connection among mentor and contender goes past the prompt domain of sports, including an association based on trust, regard, and a common obligation to individual and expert development.

7. **Versatility and Advancement:**

Abdulmanap's instructing style is described by flexibility and development. While well established in conventional Dagestani wrestling, he exhibits an eagerness to coordinate current preparation procedures. This versatility exhibits a powerful methodology that consolidates the qualities of custom with the advantages of contemporary games science. Abdulmanap's instructing style isn't stale; it advances with the times, guaranteeing that his warriors get the most ideal preparation for outcome in the always developing scene of MMA.

This versatility likewise reaches out to his inventive ways to deal with preparing, mixing customary strategies with contemporary methods. Abdulmanap's instructing style includes remaining at the front of headways in sports science, a responsibility that mirrors his devotion to giving the best preparation to his warriors. This mix of custom and development makes a training style that is both established in legacy and prepared for the difficulties of the present and future.

8. **Customized Approach:**

Abdulmanap's instructing style is recognized by his customized approach. He perceives the novel qualities, shortcomings, and properties of every contender, fitting preparation regimens to suit individual requirements. This customized consideration cultivates a profound association among mentor and contender, taking into consideration a more significant comprehension of every competitor's true capacity. Abdulmanap's instructing style includes fostering a contender's specialized abilities as well as opening their maximum capacity by tending to their particular prerequisites.

The customized approach additionally stretches out to the psychological and profound prosperity of his contenders. Abdulmanap comprehends that the mental part of contest is essentially as urgent as actual planning. His instructing style includes offering the important help and direction to assist contenders with exploring the tensions of the game. This comprehensive methodology guarantees that warriors under his tutelage are actually ready as well as intellectually versatile, adding to their general progress in the octagon.

9. **Constant Learning:**

Abdulmanap's instructing style typifies a promise to nonstop learning. In spite of his broad experience and achievement, he stays open to novel thoughts, preparing strategies, and progressions in sports science.

This devotion to remaining informed about the most recent improvements in the realm of MMA features a training style that is dynamic and ground breaking. Abdulmanap's ability to adjust and learn mirrors his real energy for the game and his craving to give the most ideal direction to his warriors.

This obligation to nonstop advancing likewise impacts his instructing staff and the more extensive MMA people group. Abdulmanap's training style includes imparting information and bits of knowledge to individual mentors, adding to the general development of training rehearses in the game. His receptiveness to learning establishes a climate where development and improvement are esteemed, guaranteeing that the contenders under his direction benefit from the most recent progressions in preparing approaches.

10. **Showing others how its done:**

Abdulmanap's training style incorporates showing others how its done. He doesn't simply teach his contenders from the sidelines; he effectively partakes in instructional courses, exhibiting methods and displaying the hard working attitude he anticipates from his competitors. This involved methodology makes a culture of common regard and shared exertion inside the rec center. Contenders under Abdulmanap's direction see a mentor as a the well as a coach standards of difficult work, discipline, and devotion. Showing others how its done stretches out past the rec center to life beyond combative techniques. Abdulmanap's own life process, set apart by difficulties and wins, turns into a wellspring of motivation for his contenders. His instructing style includes bestowing specialized abilities as well as life illustrations drawn from his encounters. This mentorship as a visual demonstration makes a significant effect on the contenders, forming their points of view as competitors as well as people exploring the intricacies of life.

11. **Accentuation on Custom:**

Abdulmanap's training style puts a critical accentuation on custom. While coordinating present day preparing systems, he guarantees that customary Dagestani wrestling procedures stay at the center of his training reasoning. This obligation to custom goes past protecting social legacy; it is an essential decision in view of the conviction that the immortal viability of conventional methods adds to the progress of his warriors.

The accentuation on custom likewise encourages a feeling of character and pride among his contenders. Abdulmanap's instructing style includes imparting a profound appreciation for Dagestani hand to hand fighting legacy, making an association among over a significant time span. This feeling of personality turns into a wellspring of solidarity for warriors, ingraining a versatility and pride that rises above the quick difficulties of contest.

12. **Long haul Improvement:**

Abdulmanap's training style focuses on long haul improvement over convenient solutions. He perceives that outcome in MMA isn't just about quick triumphs yet supported greatness over a competitor's profession. His training style includes putting resources into the extensive improvement of his warriors, guaranteeing that they have the right stuff, mentality, and strength for persevering through progress.

This drawn out advancement approach is obvious in the professions of warriors under his direction, like Khabib Nurmagomedov. The supported outcome of his contenders mirrors Abdulmanap's training style, which centers around building an establishment for enduring accomplishments as opposed to seeking after momentary increases. This obligation to long haul advancement recognizes his training reasoning and adds to the getting through traditions of the warriors he coaches.

13. **Lowliness and Humbleness:**

Lowliness and humbleness are basic parts of Abdulmanap's training style. In spite of his huge accomplishments and the outcome of his contenders, he keeps a modest disposition. This lowliness makes a good and cooperative air inside the rec center, where contenders feel esteemed and regarded. Abdulmanap's instructing style includes ingraining the specialized abilities of combative techniques as well as the ideals of humility and an appreciation for constant improvement.

This lowliness stretches out to the congeniality of Abdulmanap as a mentor and guide. Contenders under his direction feel open to looking for counsel and direction, cultivating open correspondence inside the group. The shortfall of self image in Abdulmanap's training style makes a culture where everybody, no matter what their degree of involvement, feels part of a common excursion toward greatness.

Basically, Abdulmanap Nurmagomedov's instructing style is a multilayered embroidery woven with customized consideration, a promise to nonstop getting the hang of, showing others how its done, an accentuation on custom, and an emphasis on long haul improvement. His instructing standards and values shape fruitful warriors as well as add to the more extensive scene of MMA training. Abdulmanap's effect rises above the octagon, leaving a permanent inheritance that mirrors the substance of combative techniques as a comprehensive excursion of discipline, regard, solidarity, social conservation, and consistent development.

6.3 Reflections on how these philosophies continue to resonate with fighters and fans.

Abdulmanap Nurmagomedov's methods of reasoning, profoundly implanted in discipline, regard, solidarity, social protection, comprehensive turn of events, paternal direction, versatility, customized approach, consistent getting the hang of, showing others how its done, accentuation

on custom, long haul improvement, and modesty, keep on resonating inside the domains of blended combative techniques (MMA). These core values molded his instructing style as well as enduringly affect warriors and resounded significantly with fans, making a heritage that stretches out past the triumphs inside the octagon.

Abdulmanap's ways of thinking, especially discipline and regard, have become characterizing attributes of warriors under his tutelage. The trained methodology imparted by Abdulmanap is obvious in the fastidious arrangement and enduring responsibility showed by contenders like Khabib Nurmagomedov. The accentuation on regard, for rivals as well as for the actual game, has set a norm for sportsmanship inside MMA. The getting through picture of Khabib helping a fallen rival or showing lowliness in triumph mirrors these guiding principle, resounding with fans who value the specialized ability as well as the uprightness of the warriors.

The way of thinking of solidarity, both inside the rec center and on the worldwide stage, keeps on motivating contenders and fans the same. Abdulmanap's vision of a unified Dagestani front, rising above ethnic and semantic varieties, reflects the variety of MMA itself. Contenders prepared by Abdulmanap, addressing different foundations and ethnicities, become ministers for an aggregate character. This solidarity isn't just a wellspring of solidarity inside the exercise center however a portrayal of the more extensive worldwide local area that MMA incorporates.

Social protection stays a piercing topic that reverberates with fans and contenders the same. Abdulmanap's obligation to saving customary Dagestani wrestling strategies is a demonstration of the meaning of social legacy. Fans value the profundity and genuineness brought to the game through this social reconciliation. Contenders, thusly, discover a feeling of personality and pride in conveying forward extremely old strategies, adding to the rich embroidery of hand to hand fighting history.

The all encompassing improvement reasoning, stressing mental, profound, and otherworldly development close by actual ability, makes warriors who are gifted competitors as well as balanced people. Fans associate with the narratives of warriors who, under Abdulmanap's direction, explore life's difficulties with strength and effortlessness. The possibility that combative techniques is a groundbreaking excursion goes past the energy of contest, resounding with crowds who look for stories of individual victory and development.

Paternal direction is a one of a kind part of Abdulmanap's ways of thinking that reverberates significantly with contenders. The mentorship and backing given by Abdulmanap stretch out past the exercise center, deeply shaping the existences of his contenders. This protective job makes a bond that fans can feel for, rising above the customary mentor competitor relationship. The stories of contenders recognizing Abdulmanap's impact on their vocations as well as on their own lives inspire a feeling of familial association that resounds with fans universally.

The flexibility and advancement implanted in Abdulmanap's methods of reasoning mirror a comprehension of the developing scene of MMA. Fans value the dynamism brought to the game through mentors who embrace groundbreaking thoughts and advancements. Abdulmanap's readiness to coordinate current preparation systems while safeguarding custom grandstands a fair methodology that reverberates with crowds anxious to observe the development of hand to hand fighting.

Abdulmanap's customized way to deal with training makes accounts that fans can sincerely put resources into. The narratives of warriors conquering individual difficulties and arriving at their true capacity under his direction become persuasive stories that resound with a wide crowd. The customized consideration given to every warrior, perceiving their remarkable assets and shortcomings, adds to a feeling of credibility that fans esteem in the game.

Nonstop learning, a way of thinking imbued in Abdulmanap's training style, reverberates with fans who value a pledge to greatness. The quest for information and the readiness to adjust to new data make a story of development and progress that fans view as convincing. Abdulmanap's impact stretches out not exclusively to his warriors yet in addition to the more extensive MMA people group, where mentors and lovers embrace the way of thinking of persistent improvement.

Showing others how its done is a strong part of Abdulmanap's training reasoning that resounds with fans looking for legitimacy in their legends. The picture of a mentor effectively partaking in instructional courses, exhibiting procedures, and displaying areas of strength for an ethic sets a norm of commitment that fans respect. This involved methodology makes a culture inside the rec center that fans see as certifiable and motivating.

The accentuation on custom adds to a feeling of sentimentality and realness that resounds with fanatics of hand to hand fighting. In a quickly impacting world, where sports develop at a fast speed, the protection of conventional procedures gives an association with the foundations of hand to hand fighting. Fans value the mixing of old and new, making a story that spans ages and cultivates an appreciation for the immortal parts of the game.

Long haul improvement, a critical way of thinking of Abdulmanap, makes stories of supported achievement that resound with fans looking past transient victories. The vocations of warriors under his direction become adventures of constancy, development, and persevering through greatness. Fans put sincerely in the excursions of contenders who epitomize the standards of long haul improvement, making a feeling of faithfulness and reverence for both the mentor and the competitors.

Modesty and humbleness, fundamental parts of Abdulmanap's methods of reasoning, reverberate with fans who look for genuineness in their donning legends.

The shortfall of inner self and the rational disposition of Abdulmanap and his contenders make stories that fans see as interesting. The tales of win over difficulty, combined with a feeling of lowliness, add to a story that fans interface with on a human level.

Abdulmanap Nurmagomedov's ways of thinking have made a permanent imprint on the scene of blended combative techniques (MMA), rising above the bounds of the octagon to reverberate profoundly with warriors and fans the same. The getting through effect of these ways of thinking isn't only bound to the specialized parts of preparing or the quest for triumphs; rather, they weave a story of social lavishness, self-awareness, and aggregate character that reaches out past the domain of sports.

Discipline, one of the central mainstays of Abdulmanap's methods of reasoning, keeps on being a directing power for warriors who have strolled the way he spread out. Fans observer the epitome of discipline in the relentless responsibility of warriors to their art, sticking to thorough preparation timetables and stretching their physical and mental boundaries. This obligation to teach turns into a wellspring of motivation, reverberating with fans who value the commitment expected for greatness in any undertaking.

Regard, one more foundation of Abdulmanap's lessons, penetrates the ethos of the warriors who convey his inheritance forward. The profound regard for adversaries, mentors, authorities, and the actual game establishes a climate of sportsmanship that fans see as reviving. In reality as we know it where rivalry can frequently be defaced by enmity, the showcase of certified regard turns into a guide of trustworthiness, drawing fans who value the human parts of athletic undertaking.

Solidarity, a way of thinking that Abdulmanap ingrained both inside his rec center and on the worldwide stage, reverberates as a strong story of fortitude and mutual perspective. Fans observer contenders from different foundations meeting up under a shared objective, rising above social, etymological, and public contrasts. This solidarity turns into a microcosm of the more extensive MMA people group, where fans from around the world track down a common energy and fellowship in the game.

Social safeguarding, well established in Abdulmanap's training style, has made a story of realness and legacy that enthralls fans. The combination of conventional Dagestani wrestling methods not just adds profundity to the warriors' ranges of abilities yet in addition fills in as an extension between the past and the present. Fans observer a living custom inside the game, cultivating an appreciation for the rich history and social subtleties that hand to hand fighting encapsulates.

Comprehensive turn of events, underlining mental, close to home, and otherworldly development close by actual ability, resounds with fans looking for accounts of individual victory and strength.

The narratives of warriors defeating difficulties, inside the enclosure as well as throughout everyday life, make an association that goes past the outer layer of sports diversion. Fans become put resources into the excursions of these competitors, seeing them as contenders as well as people exploring the intricacies of the human experience.

Paternal direction, a special part of Abdulmanap's instructing style, adds a layer of profound profundity to the stories of contenders. Fans observer the specialized changes as well as the self-awareness and mentorship that contenders get. This protective job makes a storyline of mentorship and familial bonds that fans can genuinely interface with, rising above the common mentor competitor dynamic.

Versatility and development, implanted in Abdulmanap's methods of reasoning, mirror a ground breaking approach that reverberates with fans anxious to observe the advancement of the game. The readiness to coordinate current preparation philosophies while saving custom grandstands a powerful instructing style that dazzles lovers searching for a mix of legacy and progress.

The customized way to deal with training turns into a story of individual stories, every extraordinary and convincing by its own doing. Fans observer contenders conquering individual difficulties, upheld a their particular by a mentor needs and potential. This customized consideration makes a feeling of credibility and appeal that fans view as convincing, cultivating a more profound association between the crowd and the competitors.

Nonstop learning, a way of thinking imbued in Abdulmanap's training style, makes a story of development and progress. Fans observer the progress of contenders as well as the obligation to progress and the quest for greatness. This devotion to consistent learning turns into a wellspring of motivation, empowering fans to embrace the ethos of long lasting improvement in their own interests.

Showing others how its done, a strong part of Abdulmanap's instructing style, sets a norm of devotion and hard working attitude that fans respect. The picture of a mentor effectively taking part in instructional meetings, exhibiting procedures, and displaying serious areas of strength for a to the specialty makes a culture of difficult work and steadiness that resounds with fans looking for credibility in their wearing legends.

The accentuation on custom makes stories that inspire a feeling of sentimentality and appreciation for the underlying foundations of combative techniques. Fans observer the mix of old and new, making a storyline that spans ages and encourages an appreciation for the immortal parts of the game. The accentuation on custom turns into a wellspring of pride for fans who relate to the rich legacy that hand to hand fighting epitomizes.

Long haul improvement, a vital way of thinking of Abdulmanap, makes stories of supported achievement that reverberate with fans looking past fleeting victories. The vocations of contenders become adventures of persistence, development, and getting through greatness. Fans put genuinely in the excursions of these competitors, making a feeling of steadfastness and reverence for both the mentor and the contenders.

Modesty and humbleness, vital parts of Abdulmanap's ways of thinking, resound with fans who look for realness in their wearing legends. The shortfall of inner self and the sensible attitude of Abdulmanap and his warriors make stories that fans see as appealing. The tales of win over misfortune, combined with a feeling of lowliness, add to a story that fans interface with on a human level.

Abdulmanap Nurmagomedov's methods of reasoning keep on resounding with contenders and fans, winding around an embroidery of stories that rise above the limits of game. These methods of reasoning, well established in social lavishness, self-awareness, and aggregate personality, have made a heritage that stretches out past the triumphs inside the octagon. The getting through effect of Abdulmanap's lessons lies not just in the specialized ability of his warriors yet in the narratives of discipline, regard, solidarity, social safeguarding, and persistent development that spellbind the hearts and brains of MMA aficionados around the world.

9

Chapter 7

Remembering Abdulmanap

Recalling Abdulmanap Nurmagomedov: A Heritage Past the Octagon

The tradition of Abdulmanap Nurmagomedov stretches out a long ways past the limits of the MMA octagon, reverberating in the hearts and brains of contenders, fans, and the worldwide hand to hand fighting local area. His effect rises above the triumphs and awards, making a permanent imprint on the game and the lives he contacted. As we ponder Abdulmanap's excursion, we dive into the angles that characterized his inheritance and keep on molding the scene of blended hand to hand fighting.

Abdulmanap's Training Reasoning:

At the center of Abdulmanap's heritage is his unmistakable training reasoning, a mix of conventional Dagestani wrestling, discipline, regard, and an all encompassing way to deal with competitor improvement. His instructing went past specialized abilities, stressing the significance of mental strength, regard for adversaries, and self-improvement. Contenders prepared under Abdulmanap were gifted competitors as well as people formed into trained, conscious, and balanced individuals.

Social Stewardship:

Abdulmanap's obligation to social safeguarding was a string woven into the texture of his training. Conventional Dagestani wrestling strategies, went down through ages, tracked down a home in his rec center. This social stewardship went past games; it was a cognizant work to shield and advance the rich legacy of Dagestan. Abdulmanap's rec center turned into a living storehouse of social works on, making an extension between the past and the present.

Protective Mentorship:

One of the most piercing parts of Abdulmanap's inheritance was his job as a protective figure to his contenders. Past the rec center, he gave mentorship, direction, and unflinching help. The connections framed were not simply mentor competitor elements; they were familial bonds that reached out into the individual existences of his contenders. This paternal mentorship made a feeling of having a place and dedication that went past the domain of sports.

Influence on Contenders:

Abdulmanap's effect on warriors was groundbreaking. His training ingrained values that rose above the octagon, forming the person and direct of his competitors. Warriors like Khabib Nurmagomedov arose as champions in the enclosure as well as diplomats of modesty, discipline, and regard beyond it. The effect of Abdulmanap's training reasoning resounded in the activities of his contenders, making good examples for yearning competitors.

Worldwide Acknowledgment:

Abdulmanap's impact was not restricted to Dagestan or Russia; it repeated around the world. His name became inseparable from greatness in training, drawing consideration from contenders and mentors all over the planet. Abdulmanap's rec center invited worldwide gifts looking for the insight and skill of a created mentor champions. The worldwide acknowledgment was a demonstration of the all inclusiveness of his instructing standards.

Theory of Constant Learning:

A viewpoint frequently featured in Abdulmanap's methodology was his obligation to ceaseless learning. Notwithstanding his broad experience, he stayed open to groundbreaking thoughts and developments in the steadily advancing scene of MMA. This way of thinking streamed down to his warriors, establishing a climate of never-ending development and flexibility. Abdulmanap's rec center was not a static element; it was a unique center point of learning and improvement.

Heritage in the Dagestani People group:

Abdulmanap Nurmagomedov was in excess of a mentor; he was an image of motivation and pride for the Dagestani people group. His prosperity and the accomplishments of his contenders elevated the spirits of a district frequently damaged by financial difficulties. Abdulmanap turned into an encouraging sign, displaying that greatness could rise up out of even the most difficult conditions. His inheritance keeps on moving the young people of Dagestan to perseveringly seek after their fantasies.

Accolade from Warriors:

The incredible flood of recognitions from contenders all over the planet following Abdulmanap's passing was a demonstration of the significant effect he had on people. Individual mentors, preparing accomplices, and contenders recognized his training keenness as well as the glow and insight he brought to the MMA people group. Recognitions illustrated a mentor who went past the specialized viewpoints, sustaining the soul of kinship and sportsmanship.

Challenges Confronted:

Abdulmanap's process was not without any trace of difficulties. The socio-political scene of Dagestan, combined with financial difficulties, added layers of intricacy to his training attempts. In any case, it was definitively these difficulties that formed Abdulmanap into a strong and decided figure. His capacity to explore difficulty turned into a basic piece of his heritage, rousing others to continue on despite hindrances.

Abdulmanap's Effect on Khabib Nurmagomedov:

The connection among Abdulmanap and his child, Khabib, was fundamental to both their own and proficient lives. Khabib's ascent to become one of the best MMA contenders in history was unpredictably connected to the direction and backing given by his dad. Abdulmanap's effect on Khabib went past training; it was a sign of a dad's confidence in his child's true capacity. The close to home association between them turned into a story that resounded with fans around the world.

Local area Advancement Drives:

Abdulmanap's heritage stretched out past the domain of sports into local area advancement drives. He effectively participated in projects pointed toward advancing a sound way of life, training, and actual wellness in Dagestan. These drives were tied in with creating first class competitors as well as about sustaining an age with upsides of discipline, regard, and a guarantee to individual prosperity.

Abdulmanap's Charity:

A less popular part of Abdulmanap's inheritance was his generous work. He upheld different worthy missions, adding to the improvement of the local area. This charity reflected his conviction that achievement ought to be shared and utilized for everyone's benefit. Abdulmanap's commitments went past the singular triumphs of his warriors; they stretched out to elevating the local area that upheld him.

The Worldwide MMA People group Grieves:

Abdulmanap's inauspicious going sent shockwaves through the worldwide MMA people group. Warriors, mentors, and fans from different corners of the world grieved the passing of a become a venerated figure name in the game. The solidarity showed in the aggregate despondency displayed the general regard and reverence Abdulmanap had gathered all through his profession.

Heritage in Schooling:

Abdulmanap's obligation to schooling as a basic piece of competitor improvement left an enduring heritage. Grants gave to promising understudies featured his faith in the cooperative energy among scholarly and actual pursuits. Abdulmanap's rec center was not only a preparation ground for contenders; it was an establishment that encouraged comprehensive turn of events, stressing the significance of balanced instruction.

Abdulmanap's Insight:

The insight granted by Abdulmanap, both all through the exercise center, turned into a directing light for those he tutored. His statements and lessons reflected the specialized subtleties of hand to hand fighting as well as significant bits of knowledge into life's difficulties. Abdulmanap's words keep on reverberating with contenders and fans, typifying the pith of discipline, regard, and the determined quest for greatness.

Abdulmanap's Soul Lives On:

While Abdulmanap Nurmagomedov may never again be genuinely present, his soul carries on with on in the endless lives he contacted. His heritage resonates in the triumphs of his warriors, the motivation he gave hoping for competitors, and the extraordinary effect he had on the MMA scene. Abdulmanap's story is a demonstration of the persevering through force of mentorship, social pride, and the unstoppable soul of a the mentor limits of sports.

7.1 A tribute to Abdulmanap Nurmagomedov's enduring legacy.

A Recognition for Abdulmanap Nurmagomedov's Getting through Inheritance

The tradition of Abdulmanap Nurmagomedov isn't simply an assortment of triumphs in the MMA field; it is an embroidery woven with strings of discipline, social extravagance, mentorship, and versatility. As we honor this wonderful mentor and visionary, we dig into the different features that characterize his getting through inheritance and the permanent imprint he has left on the universe of blended combative techniques and then some.

1. **Social Preserver:**

   Abdulmanap Nurmagomedov remains as a social preserver, meshing the customary Dagestani wrestling methods into the actual texture of his training reasoning. The meaning of this social combination goes past the specialized parts of combative techniques; it turns into a demonstration of the significance of saving legacy in a quickly developing world. Abdulmanap's rec center turned into a safe-haven where the reverberations of extremely old practices tracked down reverberation chasing contemporary greatness.

2. **Planner of Champions:**

The title of "modeler of champions" befits Abdulmanap's job in molding probably the most considerable contenders in MMA history.

His training rose above the simple bestowing of strategies; it enveloped imparting upsides of discipline, regard, and a persevering hard working attitude. The heroes who rose up out of his tutelage, unmistakably his child Khabib Nurmagomedov, became talented contenders as well as diplomats of the standards Abdulmanap held dear.

3. **Protective Figure:**

Abdulmanap's instructing stretched out a long ways past the limits of the rec center; it was a paternal direction that etched athletic ability as well as character. His warriors weren't simply aspect of a group; they were individuals from a more distant family. The close to home bonds fashioned under Abdulmanap's mentorship made stories of family relationship and devotion, cultivating a climate where people thrived as contenders as well as better individuals.

4. **Influence on Dagestani Character:**

In the complex socio-political scene of Dagestan, Abdulmanap arose as an image of trust and pride. His prosperity and the triumphs of his warriors filled in as a wellspring of motivation for a locale wrestling with monetary difficulties and social intricacies. Abdulmanap's effect stretched out past games; it turned into a story of versatility, displaying that greatness could rise out of even the most difficult conditions.

5. **Pioneer in Training:**

Abdulmanap's obligation to training as a vital piece of competitor improvement checked him as a pioneer. His accentuation on grant programs for promising understudies reflected a faith in the harmonious connection among scholarly and actual pursuits. Abdulmanap's exercise center turned into an all encompassing foundation, supporting warriors as well as balanced people with a commitment to nonstop learning.

6. **Giver on a basic level:**

Past the spotlight of the octagon, Abdulmanap was a giver on a basic level. His commitments to different worthy missions featured a conviction that achievement ought to be an impetus for positive change. This charity reflected the modesty and liberality that characterized Abdulmanap, displaying that his effect stretched out a long ways past individual triumphs to the improvement of the more extensive local area.

7. **Flexibility in Difficulty:**

Abdulmanap's process was set apart by flexibility notwithstanding affliction. The difficulties presented by the socio-political environment and financial difficulties of Dagestan didn't deflect him; all things considered, they became venturing stones for his climb. Abdulmanap's capacity to explore these difficulties turned into a vital piece of his heritage, rousing contenders and aficionados the same to endure chasing after their fantasies.

8. **Solidarity in Variety:**

Abdulmanap's rec center was a microcosm of solidarity in variety. Warriors from different foundations, identities, and ethnicities figured out something worth agreeing on under his direction. This solidarity was not just about fellowship inside the rec center; it mirrored the more extensive worldwide MMA people group, where people from different foundations joined under a common love for the game. Abdulmanap's inheritance turned into a story of solidarity rising above limits.

9. **Shrewdness Past the Enclosure:**
Abdulmanap's insight stretched out past the specialized subtleties of hand to hand fighting; it was a directing light for those he tutored. His statements and lessons reflected significant bits of knowledge into life's difficulties, discipline, and the quest for greatness. These pearls of shrewdness keep on reverberating with contenders and fans, typifying the quintessence of Abdulmanap's instructing reasoning.

10. **Worldwide Acknowledgment:**
Abdulmanap's effect rose above topographical limits, collecting worldwide acknowledgment for his training ability. Warriors and mentors overall looked to comprehend and integrate components of his exceptional instructing theory. Abdulmanap turned into a respected figure in Dagestan or Russia as well as in the more extensive MMA scene, making a permanent imprint on the game's worldwide development.

11. **Inheritance Past MMA:**
While Abdulmanap's heritage is immovably established in MMA, its branches reach out past the domain of sports. His lessons of discipline, regard, and social pride have affected people from different backgrounds. Abdulmanap's heritage turns into a reference point for anybody taking a stab at self-improvement, versatility, and a pledge to protecting social character despite change.

12. **Mentorship in Ceaselessness:**
Abdulmanap's mentorship isn't bound to a particular time; it exists in unendingness through the warriors he trained and the standards he imparted. His heritage lives on in the accounts of champions who convey forward his lessons, guaranteeing that the effect of his training reasoning keeps on molding the eventual fate of MMA. The mentorship Abdulmanap gave turns into a living heritage, rousing ages of contenders to come.

13. **Profound Reverberation:**

Abdulmanap's inheritance conveys a profound reverberation that goes past insights and accomplishments. It is implanted in the tales of warriors beating individual difficulties, the tears shed in triumph and rout, and the victory of the human soul. The close to home association Abdulmanap fashioned with his contenders and the more extensive MMA people group turns into a demonstration of the significant effect a mentor can have on lives.

14. **The Insight of Lowliness:**

One of the characterizing parts of Abdulmanap's heritage is the insight of modesty. Notwithstanding his huge accomplishments, he remained grounded and agreeable. This modesty made a culture inside his exercise center where contenders, no matter what their height, felt esteemed and regarded. Abdulmanap's inheritance is a demonstration of the extraordinary force of driving with lowliness and the enduring effect it can have on people and networks.

15. **Everlasting Motivation:**

Abdulmanap Nurmagomedov's persevering through inheritance fills in as a timeless wellspring of motivation. It rises above the limits of time and keeps on impacting the present and shape what's in store. Contenders, mentors, and aficionados draw motivation from his life's process, his training reasoning, and the qualities he held dear. Abdulmanap's heritage isn't bound to history; a living motivation resounds in the hearts of the people who keep on leading he lit.

Abdulmanap Nurmagomedov's getting through heritage is a complex embroidery that envelops social conservation, title training, paternal mentorship, influence on character, strength in difficulty, obligation to schooling, magnanimity, solidarity in variety, shrewdness past the enclosure, worldwide acknowledgment, heritage past MMA, mentorship in unendingness, close to home reverberation, the insight of lowliness, and timeless motivation. As we honor this phenomenal figure, we perceive that Abdulmanap's inheritance reaches out a long ways past the octagon, leaving a permanent engraving on the actual soul of blended combative techniques and the innumerable lives he contacted.

7.2 Reflections from family, friends, and the MMA community on his lasting impact.

Reflections on Abdulmanap Nurmagomedov's Enduring Effect: An Embroidery Woven in Recollections

Abdulmanap Nurmagomedov's impact, both in the MMA field and in the lives he contacted, keeps on reverberating through the impressions of family, companions, and the more extensive MMA people group. As we investigate the multi-layered components of his effect, an aggregate embroidery of recollections, stories, and experiences arises, exhibiting the getting through tradition of a mentor, guide, and mentor.

1. **Family Bonds and Paternal Insight:**

   Relatives consider Abdulmanap as a mentor as well as a mainstay of solidarity inside the Nurmagomedov family. His child, Khabib, frequently shared looks at the paternal direction he got. The relational peculiarity reached out past direct relations, embracing the contenders in Abdulmanap's rec center. The insight he bestowed was not bound to instructional meetings but rather reverberated in the discussions around the supper table, making an environment of learning and backing.

2. **The Mentorship Past the Exercise center:**

   Companions and preparing accomplices illustrate Abdulmanap as a guide whose impact rose above the exercise center's limits. The mentorship he gave was not restricted to battle systems; it reached out to life illustrations, discipline, and lowliness. Warriors review minutes when Abdulmanap's recommendation directed them through private difficulties, changing the rec center into a cauldron of character improvement.

3. **Tales of Social Wealth:**

   Abdulmanap's obligation to safeguarding Dagestani culture is reflected in the memories of loved ones. Accounts arise of how he consistently incorporated customary wrestling procedures into the preparation routine, it was safeguarded as well as effectively celebrated to guarantee that social legacy. The exercise center, under his direction, turned into a social center point where warriors learned the craft of battle as well as the pith of their social roots.

4. **Influence on Contenders' Lives:**
Contenders, both current and previous, share piercing reflections on how Abdulmanap molded their lives past the octagon. The effect goes past battle records; it dives into the domains of self-awareness, flexibility, and the getting through impact of an in the expected mentor of every person. Abdulmanap's heritage is carved in the stories of warriors who arose as champions as well as people advanced by his lessons.

5. **Social Minister:**
Loved ones ponder Abdulmanap as a social representative, for Dagestan as well as for the more extensive MMA people group. His rec center turned into a blend of ability, drawing in contenders from different foundations. Through his training, Abdulmanap displayed the extravagance of Dagestani customs to the world, cultivating a feeling of satisfaction among the contenders as well as inside the worldwide MMA people group.

6. **Recollections of Wins and Difficulties:**
Pondering Abdulmanap's excursion, both loved ones share recollections of wins and difficulties. The triumphs in the enclosure are entwined with accounts of conquering difficulty, exploring the complex socio-political scene of Dagestan, and the enduring assurance that characterized his training vocation. These recollections become strings in the bigger story of a through both individual and expert mentor difficulties.

7. **Solidarity in Distress:**
The MMA people group, joined in distress, offers reflections on

the aggregate effect of Abdulmanap's passing. Individual mentors, warriors, and fans express a common feeling of misfortune, stressing the void left by a figure whose impact reached out a long ways past his nearby circles. The solidarity in sadness turns into a piercing demonstration of the worldwide acknowledgment and regard Abdulmanap earned all through his profession.

8. **Tradition of Shrewdness:**

Loved ones share pieces of Abdulmanap's insight, frequently exemplified in important statements and lessons. His sayings go past the details of the game, offering significant bits of knowledge into life, discipline, and the quest for greatness. These pearls of shrewdness, reverberated by the people who prepared under him, keep on resounding as core values for warriors and people the same.

9. **Commitments to Local area:**

Loved ones shed light on Abdulmanap's commitments to local area improvement. Drives pointed toward advancing a solid way of life, training, and actual wellness arise as fundamental pieces of his heritage. The effect on the more extensive local area becomes apparent through accounts of grants gave, offices constructed, and the positive impact applied on the existences of those external the quick circle of MMA.

10. **Generosity and Offering in return:**

A frequently disregarded part of Abdulmanap's heritage is his generous work. Loved ones relate cases of his liberality, supporting different worthy missions to improve the local area. This generosity, driven by a faith in offering in return, turns into a necessary piece of the story, displaying that achievement, in Abdulmanap's eyes, stretched out past private accomplishments to elevating those out of luck.

11. **Interviews with Previous Understudies:**

Previous understudies, presently fruitful warriors and mentors by their own doing, offer inside and out experiences into

Abdulmanap's instructing techniques. They dive into the subtleties of preparing regimens, the accentuation on mental backbone, and the customized approach that characterized his training style. These meetings give a window into the profundity of Abdulmanap's effect on individual professions and the more extensive scene of MMA training.

12. **Thinking back Instructional courses:**

Relatives and preparing accomplices share distinctive memories of instructional meetings under Abdulmanap's careful attention. The power of exercises is combined with stories of giggling, brotherhood, and the interesting mix of discipline and warmth that characterized the environment. These memories become windows into the day to day schedules that manufactured contenders as well as a closely knit local area inside the rec center.

13. **Recognitions from the MMA People group:**

Recognitions from the more extensive MMA people group, including warriors, mentors, and associations, lay out an aggregate representation of regard and esteem. From web-based entertainment presents on open proclamations, the recognitions feature the significant effect Abdulmanap had on the game. The reverberation of his heritage is clear in the expressions of the people who might not have prepared straightforwardly under him yet felt the far reaching influences of his impact.

14. **Tributes of Self-improvement:**

Previous warriors share tributes of self-awareness catalyzed by Abdulmanap's training. Past the actual changes, these accounts describe excursions of self-disclosure, flexibility, and the soaking up of values that stretch out a long ways past the bounds of the enclosure. Abdulmanap's training turns into an extraordinary power that shapes vocations as well as whole lives.

15. **The Profound Reverberation of Misfortune:**

Family, companions, and the MMA people group express the profound reverberation of Abdulmanap's misfortune. The anguish rises above the expert domain, taking advantage of the profoundly special interactions manufactured over long periods of shared wins and difficulties. The close to home embroidery painted by the people who realized him personally turns into a demonstration of the significant effect a mentor can have on the existences of his contenders and the local area at large.

The reflections from family, companions, and the MMA people group structure a rich embroidery that embodies Abdulmanap Nurmagomedov's persevering through heritage. From the familial bonds and protective insight to the effect on contenders' lives, the conservation of social extravagance, and the worldwide acknowledgment he earned, these reflections offer looks into the diverse components of a mentor whose impact stretches out a long ways past the limits of sports. As recollections entwine and tales meet, Abdulmanap's enduring effect turns into an aggregate story that keeps on molding the universe of blended combative techniques and move ages to come.

7.3 Examining how his teachings continue to inspire future generations of fighters.

Abdulmanap Nurmagomedov's Persevering through Impact: Rousing the Eventual fate of MMA

Abdulmanap Nurmagomedov's lessons and reasoning have risen above reality, making an enduring effect that resounds with current warriors and keeps on moving the yearnings of people in the future in the powerful universe of Blended Hand to hand fighting (MMA). As we dive into the assessment of how his heritage perseveres, we reveal the manners by which Abdulmanap's lessons act as a directing light, molding the ethos and desires of warriors who emulate his example.

1. **Development of Discipline and Hard working attitude:**
   At the core of Abdulmanap's training reasoning falsehoods a resolute accentuation on discipline and hard working attitude.

These central standards are implanted in the texture of his lessons, making an establishment whereupon people in the future of warriors fabricate their vocations. Contenders who prepared under Abdulmanap frequently discuss the thorough preparation schedules and the assumption for tireless devotion to the art.

This development of discipline and hard working attitude turns into a foundation that hoists individual execution as well as sets a norm for hopeful warriors to copy.

2. **Mentality of Ceaseless Learning:**

Abdulmanap's way to deal with instructing reached out past the specialized parts of battling; it embraced a mentality of ceaseless learning. Contenders under his tutelage were shown explicit strategies as well as were urged to develop and adjust. This way of thinking turns into an impetus for development inside the game, cultivating an age of contenders who approach their specialty with a receptiveness to groundbreaking thoughts and a promise to persistent improvement. Abdulmanap's heritage, in such manner, fills in as a reference point for contenders to see their vocations as a continuous excursion of development.

3. **Reconciliation of Mental Sturdiness:**

MMA is however much a psychological distraction as it could be physical, and Abdulmanap perceived this inherent association. His lessons accentuate the significance of mental durability, strength, and the capacity to defeat misfortune. Contenders who convey forward his inheritance frequently trait their psychological mettle to the illustrations learned under Abdulmanap's direction. This joining of mental sturdiness turns into a main trait that helps warriors inside the enclosure as well as prepares them to explore the difficulties past it.

4. **Accentuation on Regard and Sportsmanship:**

One of the particular highlights of Abdulmanap's instructing reasoning is the accentuation on regard and sportsmanship. In a game known for its power and seriousness, he imparted values that rose above simple triumph. Contenders who prepared with Abdulmanap convey forward a tradition of carefully maintaining regard for rivals, authorities, and the actual game. This accentuation on sportsmanship shapes the singular person of warriors as well as adds to the general ethos of MMA as a game established in shared regard.

5. **Utilization of Customary Hand to hand fighting:**
Abdulmanap's exceptional methodology includes the reconciliation of conventional Dagestani wrestling procedures into the cutting edge MMA scene. This combination of customary and contemporary hand to hand fighting turns into a sign of his instructing style. Warriors who embrace these procedures gain a specialized benefit as well as add to the conservation and development of conventional practices inside the unique setting of MMA. Abdulmanap's lessons, thusly, overcome any issues between the rich history of combative techniques and its state of the art present.

6. **Tradition of Paternal Mentorship:**
The paternal mentorship that Abdulmanap gave stretches out as a living heritage that moves the familial bonds inside MMA exercise centers. Warriors who prepared under Abdulmanap frequently portray the exercise center climate as a more distant family, with the mentor expecting a protective job.
This tradition of mentorship and familial securities adds to a strong and sustaining climate inside the MMA people group, empowering future warriors to look for greatness in their specialty as well as cultivate significant associations with their mentors and preparing accomplices.

7. **Influence on Social Personality:**
Abdulmanap's lessons stretch out past the details of battling; they become a wellspring of social character for contenders from Dagestan and then some. The fuse of customary wrestling strategies and the festival of social extravagance inside the exercise

center make a remarkable personality for contenders. This feeling of social pride turns into a main thrust that rouses warriors to succeed separately as well as add to the more extensive story of social portrayal inside MMA.

8. **Instructive Concentration:**
Abdulmanap's obligation to instruction as a necessary piece of competitor improvement is an inheritance that shapes the desires of future warriors. The grants and instructive projects he started feature the significance of scholarly development close by actual ability. Contenders propelled by Abdulmanap's heritage comprehend that progress in MMA isn't just about triumphs in the enclosure yet in addition about all encompassing turn of events, underlining the worth of schooling as a pathway to individual and expert satisfaction.

9. **Charity as a Core value:**
The charitable undertakings supported by Abdulmanap act as a core value for future contenders. The idea that achievement ought to be shared for the long term win turns into an uplifting component inside the MMA people group. Contenders who line up with Abdulmanap's heritage perceive the potential for positive effect past individual accomplishments, driving an aggregate liability to add to local area improvement and generosity.

10. **Worldwide Acknowledgment and Reach:**
Abdulmanap's worldwide acknowledgment as a mentor of unmatched mastery makes an optimistic objective for warriors around the world. The exercise center he laid out turned into an objective for worldwide gifts trying to prepare under a mentor of his type. This worldwide acknowledgment extends the skylines for future warriors, empowering them to see MMA as a nearby pursuit as well as a game with the potential for worldwide effect.

11. **Building a Heritage Past the Octagon:**
Contenders enlivened by Abdulmanap's inheritance comprehend the significance of building a heritage that stretches out

past the limits of the octagon. The triumphs accomplished inside the enclosure become venturing stones for a more extensive story of social protection, mentorship, and positive impact inside the local area. This acknowledgment propels future contenders to imagine their vocations as a quest for individual brilliance as well as a chance to contribute seriously to the game and society.

12. **The Close to home Association with Abdulmanap's Heritage:** Future warriors frequently express a close to home association with Abdulmanap's inheritance, regardless of whether they haven't straightforwardly prepared under him. The narratives of flexibility, the familial bonds inside the rec center, and the getting through influence on individual lives make a close to home reverberation that rises above geological and generational limits. This close to home association turns into a main thrust, moving contenders to encapsulate the standards and values supported by Abdulmanap.

13. **Advancing Variety and Incorporation:** Abdulmanap's heritage advances variety and incorporation inside the MMA people group. Warriors from different foundations, identities, and ethnicities tracked down a home in his rec center, separating obstructions and cultivating a feeling of solidarity. This inclusivity turns into a model for future warriors, empowering them to embrace the variety inside the game and add to a climate that invites people from varying backgrounds.

14. **The Insight of Modesty:** The insight of modesty conferred by Abdulmanap fills in as a directing light for future warriors. Despite accomplishments and honors, embracing lowliness turns into a primary rule. This lowliness adds to a positive rec center culture as well as shapes the personality of warriors, making good examples who approach accomplishment with elegance and regard for the excursion.

15. **Propagating Abdulmanap's Methods of reasoning:** The propagation of Abdulmanap's ways of thinking lies in the

possession of current contenders and mentors who have guzzled his lessons. As they rise to influential positions inside rec centers and the more extensive MMA people group, they become torchbearers of his heritage. The obligation to guarantee that the standards of discipline, regard, social pride, and charity get through turns into an aggregate undertaking, getting Abdulmanap's heritage for people in the future.

16. **Local area Commitment and Grassroots Turn of events:**
A basic part of Abdulmanap's persevering through impact is his obligation to local area commitment and grassroots turn of events. Future warriors are roused not just by his progress in the world class MMA circuit yet in addition by the grassroots drives that plan to support ability from the very establishments. Abdulmanap's heritage is portrayed by the production of pathways for hopeful warriors at the local area level, offering valuable open doors for expertise advancement and mentorship in districts where MMA probably won't have been as available.

17. **Advancement in Preparing Techniques:**
Abdulmanap was known for his inventive way to deal with preparing techniques, continuously looking for ways of streamlining execution and improve the range of abilities of his contenders.
This obligation to development turns into a wellspring of motivation for future warriors who comprehend that remaining at the very front of the game requires a readiness to adjust and develop. Whether it's consolidating new advances or refining conventional procedures, Abdulmanap's heritage supports a mentality of constant development in preparing strategies.

18. **Ecological Versatility:**
Warriors who draw motivation from Abdulmanap's inheritance perceive the significance of ecological flexibility. The preparation regimens in Dagestan, frequently under testing conditions, impart a feeling of versatility and flexibility. This part of Abdulmanap's training turns into a significant illustration for warriors

who might confront changed conditions and conditions all through their professions. The capacity to flourish in various settings and conditions turns into a demonstration of the flexibility imparted by Abdulmanap's lessons.

19. **Tradition of Abdulmanap's Heritage:**
As warriors progress in their vocations, they become the living tradition of Abdulmanap's heritage. The effect they have on the game, the qualities they epitomize, and the positive impact they apply inside the MMA people group become expansions of the inheritance he made. Future contenders are not simply motivated by Abdulmanap's lessons; they try to add to the continuous story of his inheritance, guaranteeing that the standards he advocated keep on molding the game for a long time into the future.

20. **Reception of an All encompassing Methodology:**
Abdulmanap's training theory embraced a comprehensive way to deal with competitor improvement, taking into account actual ability as well as mental and profound prosperity. Future warriors perceive the significance of equilibrium in their lives, understanding that outcome in the enclosure is interconnected with generally prosperity. Abdulmanap's heritage, consequently, turns into an outline for a comprehensive methodology that envelops actual wellness, mental flexibility, and profound wellbeing.

21. **Authority Past the Exercise center:**
The initiative characteristics exhibited by Abdulmanap stretch out past the exercise center setting. Future warriors are propelled by his training discernment as well as by his capacity to show others how its done in different parts of life. From exploring difficulties in a wild socio-political environment to adding to local area improvement, Abdulmanap's initiative fills in as a guide for contenders to perceive the more extensive obligations that accompany their foundation as competitors.

22. **Encouraging an Affection for the Game:**
Abdulmanap's energy for MMA was infectious, and future

warriors are inspired by his capacity to impart a certifiable love for the game. The delight he tracked down in training, the brotherhood inside the exercise center, and the festival of triumphs both of all shapes and sizes add to an environment where the affection for MMA turns into a main thrust.

Future contenders try not exclusively to prevail in that frame of mind to sustain a profound and persevering through enthusiasm for the game.

23. **Social Trade and Worldwide Mix:**
Abdulmanap's inheritance is set apart by a feeling of social trade and worldwide coordination inside the MMA people group. Future warriors perceive the significance of embracing assorted viewpoints, preparing with people from various foundations, and adding to a game that rises above geological limits. Abdulmanap's rec center, with its global program of contenders, turns into a model for encouraging social trade inside the MMA world.

24. **Engaging Ladies in MMA:**
While Abdulmanap's inheritance principally spins around male warriors, people in the future are enlivened to grow the inclusivity of the game. The standards of discipline, regard, and difficult work are widespread, and future warriors are headed to add to the strengthening of ladies in MMA. This advancement lines up with the changing scene of the game, recognizing the basic job that ladies play in forming the fate of MMA.

25. **Tradition of Life Examples:**
Past the specialized parts of battling, Abdulmanap's inheritance is a storehouse of life examples. Future contenders are attracted to the insight implanted in his lessons — illustrations of lowliness, steadiness, and the quest for greatness in all parts of life. Abdulmanap's heritage turns into an aide for effective professions in MMA as well as for exploring the intricacies of existence with effortlessness and uprightness.

26. **Adjusting to Present day Difficulties:**
Abdulmanap's training reasoning exhibited a capacity to adjust to present day challenges. Future warriors perceive the significance of remaining applicable in a consistently developing games scene. Whether it's changing preparation techniques to integrate mechanical headways or exploring the intricacies of online entertainment, Abdulmanap's heritage rouses a proactive way to deal with tending to the difficulties of the cutting edge period.

27. **The Quest for Greatness in Character:**
While triumphs in the enclosure are commended, future warriors are spurred by Abdulmanap's accentuation on the quest for greatness in character. The characteristics of lowliness, regard, and thoughtfulness are as necessary to his inheritance as title belts. Contenders motivated by Abdulmanap comprehend that their effect goes past the limits of rivalry; it stretches out to the positive impact they can apply on people and networks through their personality.

28. **Instructive Drives as an Impetus:**
The instructive drives supported by Abdulmanap become an impetus so that future warriors might be able to see past the prompt satisfaction of triumphs.

The grants and instructive projects mirror a guarantee to long haul influence, empowering contenders to see their professions as vehicles for more extensive cultural commitments. Abdulmanap's heritage, subsequently, turns into a main impetus for contenders to put resources into their schooling and influence their foundation for positive change.

29. **Inheritance as a Bringing together Power:**
Abdulmanap's inheritance fills in as a binding together power inside the MMA people group. Contenders enlivened by his lessons perceive that, regardless of individual affiliations, they share an ongoing idea — a guarantee to the standards he supported. This feeling of solidarity turns into a strong power for good change

inside the game, encouraging a climate where competitions in the enclosure coincide with shared regard outside it.

30. **An Enduring Image of Motivation:**

As future warriors leave on their excursions in the realm of MMA, Abdulmanap's heritage stays an enduring image of motivation. His biography, training reasoning, and the effect he had on people reverberate as a wellspring of inspiration for the people who try to transform the game. The reverberations of his impact resonate through preparing rec centers, storage spaces, and fields, making a heritage that rises above the limits of existence.

The assessment of how Abdulmanap Nurmagomedov's lessons keep on moving people in the future of warriors uncovers a rich embroidery woven with strings of local area commitment, development, ecological versatility, the propagation of his heritage, an all encompassing methodology, administration past the exercise center, an affection for the game, social trade, strengthening of ladies, life examples, adjusting to present day challenges, greatness in character, instructive drives, a binding together power, and an enduring image of motivation. Abdulmanap's impact perseveres through not just in that frame of mind of his past warriors however in the yearnings and tries of the people who convey forward his lessons into the consistently advancing domain of MMA.